Paul—His Life, Letters, and Teaching

PAUL

His Life, Letters, and Teaching

Convenient Summaries

Murray J. Harris

 CASCADE *Books* • Eugene, Oregon

PAUL—HIS LIFE, LETTERS, AND TEACHING
Convenient Summaries

Copyright © 2022 Murray J. Harris. All rights reserved. Except for brief quotations in critical publications or reviews, no part of this book may be reproduced in any manner without prior written permission from the publisher. Write: Permissions, Wipf and Stock Publishers, 199 W. 8th Ave., Suite 3, Eugene, OR 97401.

Cascade Books
An Imprint of Wipf and Stock Publishers
199 W. 8th Ave., Suite 3
Eugene, OR 97401

www.wipfandstock.com

PAPERBACK ISBN: 978-1-6667-3822-3
HARDCOVER ISBN: 978-1-6667-9862-3
EBOOK ISBN: 978-1-6667-9863-0

Cataloguing-in-Publication data:

Names: Harris, Murray J., author.

Title: Paul—his life, letters, and teaching : convenient summaries / by Murray J. Harris.

Description: Eugene, OR: Cascade Books, 2022

Identifiers: ISBN 978-1-6667-3822-3 (paperback) | ISBN 978-1-6667-9862-3 (hardcover) | ISBN 978-1-6667-9863-0 (ebook)

Subjects: LCSH: Paul, the Apostle, Saint. | Bible. Epistles of Paul—Criticism, interpretation, etc.

Classification: BS2650.52 H377 2022 (print) | BS2650.52 (ebook)

10/06/22

To

Geoff R. Edwards

"my true son in the faith we share" (Titus 1:4)

and to his wife Keren and their delightful family,
Jacob, Finn, and Isla

CONTENTS

List of Maps | xiv
Preface | xv
Acknowledgments | xvii
Abbreviations | xviii

I. INTRODUCTION | 1
A. Sources for Reconstructing the Life, Letters, and Teaching of Paul | 1
  1. The Acts of the Apostles 1
    (a) Authorship 1
    (b) Date 2
    (c) Audience 2
    (d) Place and Circumstances of Writing 2
    (e) Purposes 2
  2. Paul's Letters
    (a) The Extent of the Pauline Corpus 3
    (b) The Grouping of Paul's Letters 3
    (c) The Collection of Paul's Letters 5
    (d) Paul as Writer 6
  3. Relationship of Acts and Paul's Letters 8
B. Suggested Chronology of Paul's Life and Letters | 11

II. LIFE AND LETTERS OF PAUL | 14
STAGE I: From Birth to Conversion (up to AD 33) | 14

1. Time of Paul's Birth   14
2. Paul's Name and Pedigree   15
3. Paul's Persecution of Early Christians   16
4. Paul's Conversion and Call   16

STAGE II: Early Post-conversion Activity (AD 33–46) | 18

1. Damascus–Arabia–Damascus (AD 33–35) (Acts 9:1–25; Gal 1:17)   18
2. Paul's First Post-conversion Visit to Jerusalem (AD 35) (Acts 9:26–30; Gal 1:18–20)   19
3. The Ten "Silent Years" (AD 35–45)   20
4. Barnabas and Paul at Antioch (AD 45) (Acts 11:25–26)   21
5. Barnabas and Paul Travel to Jerusalem with Famine Relief (AD 46) (Acts 11:27–30)   21
6. The "Antioch Incident" (AD 46 or 47) (Gal 2:11–14)   23

STAGE III: First Missionary Journey (AD 47–48) (Acts 13:1—15:35) | 24

1. Route   24
2. Highlights   24
   (a) Paul's Traveling Companions   24
   (b) The Establishment of a Standard Evangelistic Pattern (Acts 13:5, 14; 14:1; 17:2)   26
   (c) The Conversion of Sergius Paulus in Rome-Oriented Paphos (Acts 13:6–12)   27
   (d) Paul's Leadership as the "Chief Speaker" (Acts 13:13; 14:12)   27
   (e) Ministry in Pisidian Antioch (Acts 13:13–48)   27
3. Aftermath   28
   (a) Demand of "False Believers": "No Circumcision, No Salvation" (Acts 15:1)   28
   GALATIANS (AD 48)
   (b) The Jerusalem Council (AD 49) (Acts 15:2–29)   29

CONTENTS

**STAGE IV: Second Missionary Journey (AD 49–52)
(Acts 15:36—18:22)** | 30

1. Route   30
2. Highlights   30
   (a) One Planned Expedition Becomes Two
       (Acts 15:36–41)   30
   (b) Paul's Traveling Companions   30
   (c) Movement Westward into Europe (Acts 16:6–12)   32
   (d) Conversion of Lydia and the Jailer and their House-
       holds (Acts 16:13–34)   32
   (e) Strategic Use of Roman Citizenship at Philippi
       (Acts 16:35–40)   33
   (f) Apologetics in Thessalonica (Acts 17:1–9)   33
   (g) Missionary Adaptability in Athens (Acts 17:10–34)   34
   (h) Eighteen or More Months in Corinth
       (Acts 18:1–18a)   35
3. Aftermath   36
   1 THESSALONIANS (AD 50)
   2 THESSALONIANS (AD 50)

**STAGE V: Third Missionary Journey (AD 52–57)
(Acts 18:23—21:14)** | 38

1. Route   38
2. Highlights   38
   (a) Paul's Traveling Companions   38
   (b) Christian Baptism of John the Baptist's Disciples
       (Acts 19:1–7)   40
   (c) Discussions in the Hall of Tyrannus (Acts 19:8–10)   40
   (d) Paul Sends the "Previous Letter" (1 Cor 5:9–10)   40
   (e) Disclosure and Conflagration as Proof of Genuine
       Repentance (Acts 19:13–20)   40
   1 CORINTHIANS (SPRING AD 55)

CONTENTS

(f) Paul's "Painful Visit" to Corinth (Summer or Fall AD 55)   41
(g) The Demetrius Riot (Acts 19:23–41)   42
(h) Paul's Distress in Troas and Macedonia (Spring AD 56)   42
(i) Paul's "Affliction in Asia" (Spring AD 56)   43
(j) Visit to Illyricum (Rom 15:19–21)   43
    2 CORINTHIANS (Fall AD 56)
    ROMANS (early AD 57)
(k) Delegates for the "Collection for the Poor" (Acts 20:4)   44
(l) Raising of Eutychus at Troas (Acts 20:6–12)   45
(m) Paul's farewell speech to the Ephesian elders at Miletus (Acts 20:13–38)   45
(n) To Jerusalem via Tyre and Caesarea (Acts 21:1–14)   46
(o) Paul's Five Post-conversion Visits to Jerusalem   46

STAGE VI: Journey to Rome (AD 57–62) (Acts 21:15—28:31) | 47
1. Route   47
2. Highlights   47
    (a) Paul's Traveling Companions   47
    (b) Purification Ritual in Jerusalem (Acts 21:20–26)   49
    (c) Defense before the Jerusalem Crowd (Acts 21:37—22:22)   49
    (d) Defense before the Sanhedrin (Acts 22:30—23:11)   50
    (e) Defense before Antonius Felix (Acts 24:1–27)   51
    (f) Defense before Porcius Festus and Paul's "Appeal to Caesar" (Acts 25:1–12)   52
    (g) Defense before Herod Agrippa II (Acts 25:23—26:32)   53
    (h) Storm and Shipwreck (Acts 27:13–44)   54
    (i) Reassurances at Malta (Acts 28:1–16)   55
    (j) Defense before Jewish Leaders (Acts 28:17–28)   55

(k) "Free Custody" in Rome (Acts 28:30–31)   56
    COLOSSIANS (AD 60)
    PHILEMON (AD 60)
    EPHESIANS (AD 60)
    PHILIPPIANS (AD 61)

STAGE VII: From Paul's Release from House Arrest to His Death (AD 62–64 or 65) | 58

  1. Route   58

  2. Defensible Assumptions   58

    (a) The Pastorals (1 and 2 Timothy and Titus) Were Written by Paul   58

        1 TIMOTHY (AD 63)

        TITUS (AD 63)

        2 TIMOTHY (AD 64)

    (b) Geographical References Are Accurate   60

    (c) Paul Released, Then Later Arrested   60

    (d) Alternative Views Are Less Convincing   61

  Paul as a Missionary Statesman   61

  Four Low Points in Paul's Career   63

III. TEACHING OF PAUL | 68

  A. Sources of Paul's Teaching | 68

    1. Old Testament   68

    2. Hellenism   68

    3. Christian Tradition   68

    4. Damascus Encounter with Christ   69

    5. Apostolic Experience   69

    6. Progressive Illumination of the Holy Spirit   69

  B. The Godhead | 69

    1. The Trinity   69

    2. God as Father   70

    3. God as Savior   70

4. Jesus Christ: His Person   71
   (a) His Humanity   71
   (b) His Deity   72
   (c) His Subordination to the Father   73
   (d) His Primacy as the Lord (*Kyrios*)   73
5. Jesus Christ: His work as the Father's Agent   74
   (a) Justification   74
   (b) Bearer of God's Wrath   74
   (c) Substitution   75
   (d) Propitiation and Expiation   75
   (e) Reconciliation   76
   (f) Forgiveness   76
   (g) Adoption   76
   (h) Principalities and Powers   77
   (i) Summary   77
6. The Holy Spirit   77
   (a) His roles or Functions   77
      (i) As the Spirit of God/Christ   77
      (ii) As the Spirit of Life   78
      (iii) Other Distinctive Roles   79
   (b) The Baptism and Fullness of the Spirit   79

C. Human Beings | 80
1. As Bearers of God's Image   80
2. Terms Describing the Human Person   81
3. Being "in Christ"   82

D. Images of the Church | 83
1. In Relation to God the Father   83
   (a) The People of God   83
   (b) The Temple of God   83
   (c) The Household of God   83
   (d) The New Humanity   83

2. In Relation to Christ   83
   (a) The Body of Christ   83
   (b) The Bride of Christ   83
E. Sacraments of the Church | 83
   1. Baptism   83
   2. The Lord's Supper   84
   3. The Relationship between Baptism and
      the Lord's Supper   84
F. Ethics | 85
   1. Family Relationships   85
      (a) The Husband-Wife Relationship   85
      (b) The Parent-Child Relationship   85
      (c) Relatives   85
   2. General Human Relationships   86
      (a) Interpersonal/Individual   86
      (b) Intra-Communal/Civic   86
G. Eschatology | 87
   1. Death   87
   2. The Intermediate State   87
   3. Resurrection   88
   4. Immortality   89
   5. Comparison of Paul and Plato on Immortality   90
   6. Eternal Life   95
   7. Parousia/Second Advent   96
   8. Judgment   96
   9. The Final State   97
H. Paul and the Law | 99
I. Paul and Israel | 100
J. Paul and Jesus | 103
K. Development in Paul's Thought? | 105
L. Some Modern Images of Paul | 106
M. The Center of Paul's Teaching | 107

LIST OF MAPS

1. Paul's First Missionary Journey | 25
2. Paul's Second Missionary Journey | 31
3. Paul's Third Missionary Journey | 39
4. Paul's Journey to Rome | 48

These four maps are reproduced with permission from the *Holman Book of Biblical Charts, Maps, and Reconstructions*, edited by Marsha A. Ellis Smith et al. (Nashville: Broadman and Holman, 1993), 128–31.

PREFACE

FOR SOME FORTY YEARS I have been privileged to teach courses on "Acts and Paul" and "Pauline Theology" at the undergraduate, graduate, and doctoral levels and in many different church settings. One thing I have learned from that rewarding experience is that students of all ages warmly appreciate a comprehensive overview (or "convenient summary"!) of any topic they are studying, an overview that will whet their appetite for more detailed reading or research—and help them pass exams! Hence the present book. Any teacher has achieved success who provides a broad perspective on a subject that generates fascination with the topic and a desire to learn more about it. To illustrate this point, I have included a detailed "Comparison of Paul and Plato on Immortality" after the summary of Paul's view of immortality.

So in creating the present "convenient summaries" I have tried to cultivate what I have always admired in my classical studies—a Tacitean style of writing that is condensed, succinct, and measured. Whether I have achieved my aim, the reader will have to judge. At least I hope that you will often react by thinking "That's interesting! I never realized that. I must inquire some more."

When it comes to Paul's theology, I am fully aware of the wide variety of views that his teaching has provoked. If some label my approach to be that of "informed conservatism," I would not demur. "Conservative," yes. For I assume the Pauline authorship of all thirteen letters that have traditionally been ascribed to him and find the traditional understanding of his theological thought to be defensible. "Informed," yes. For I have gingerly walked up part of the mountain of volumes about Paul's thinking, witness my listing

PREFACE

of "Some Modern Images of Paul" at the end of my summaries of his teaching—and the end of the book!

One distinctive of the book that might appeal to readers is the relative absence of footnotes that can clutter a text. Readers will need to assume that the author is aware of the issues of interpretation that arise from the text of Acts and Paul's letters, a fair assumption given the fact that the author has written a commentary of 1,110 pages on one of Paul's letters, has written a recent book on *The Church of Corinth in the First Century AD* (2022), has authored several books that deal with aspects of Paul's theology (often in the wider context of NT theology in general), and has been teaching and writing in these areas for fifty years.

Throughout the book, dates are proposed for Paul's movements and letters. Although they occur in various places in the text, they are uniform and consistent.

All translations of ancient texts are my own, unless indicated.

ACKNOWLEDGMENTS

WITH THE KIND PERMISSION of the publishers, I have made use of material, usually with changes, found in the following books: F. F. Bruce, *The Acts of the Apostles. The Greek Text with Introduction and Commentary*, 3rd ed. (Grand Rapids: Eerdmans, 1990); M. J. Harris, *Navigating Tough Texts* (Bellingham, WA: Lexham, 2020); M. J. Harris, *Raised Immortal: Resurrection and Immortality in the New Testament* (Grand Rapids: Eerdmans, 1985); and from my article "The New Testament View of Life after Death," *Themelios* 11 (1986) 47–52.

Warm gratitude is due to Broadman and Holman for permission to reproduce four maps of Paul's journeys found in the *Holman Book of Biblical Charts, Maps, and Reconstructions*, edited by Marsha A. Ellis Smith et al. (Nashville: Broadman and Holman, 1993).

I am indebted to my friend of seventy years, David Burt, for his astute comments on the manuscript that proved very helpful. Also, I gratefully acknowledge the skillful and efficient editorial work at Cascade Books of Dr. Chris Spinks, Stephanie Hough, Rebecca Abbott, and Calvin Jaffarian.

ABBREVIATIONS

BDAG	W. Bauer, *A Greek-English Lexicon of the New Testament and Other Christian Literature*, 3rd ed., edited by F. W. Danker et al. (Chicago: University of Chicago, 2000).
cf.	*confer* (Latin), compare
ESV	English Standard Version Bible (2001)
KJV	King James Version (= Authorized Version) (1611)
LXX	Septuagint (Greek version of the OT)
NASB	New American Standard Bible (1977)
NIV	New International Version (2011)
NJB	New Jerusalem Bible (1985)
NLT	New Living Translation of the Bible (2013)
NRSV	New Revised Standard Version Bible (1989)
NT	New Testament
OT	Old Testament
RV	Revised Version (New Testament) (1881)
TCNT	Twentieth Century New Testament (1904)
viz.	*videlicet* (Lat.), namely
Weymouth	R. F. Weymouth, *The New Testament in Modern Speech* (1909)

I. INTRODUCTION

IN ANY RECONSTRUCTION OF an ancient person's life and thought, an ideal situation requires a reliable and detailed historical document to provide the setting for any fair assessment of that person. In the case of the first-century AD Paul of Tarsus, we have a unique correlation between an historical document (the book of the Acts of the Apostles) and the various letters Paul wrote that enables such a trustworthy evaluation.

A. Sources for Reconstructing the Life, Letters, and Teaching of Paul

1. The Acts of the Apostles

   (a) Authorship: Luke

   - There is an identity of style and language between the four "we" passages (Acts 16:10-17 [Troas to Philippi]; 20:5-15 [Philippi to Miletus]; 21:1-18 [Miletus to Jerusalem]; 27:1—28:16 [Caesarea to Rome]) and the rest of Acts. The inference of a single author prepares the way for the next point.

   - Of all Paul's traveling companions known from his letters, Luke is the person most likely to have authored these "we" passages (assuming these passages to be eyewitness accounts). This leads us to assume that Luke is the author of Acts.

   - External evidence from the late second century AD onwards (about AD 180: Irenaeus, Muratorian Canon, anti-Marcionite prologue to Luke) is unanimous for Luke as the author of the Third Gospel and Acts.

(b) Date: AD 62–63

- The Jews are portrayed in Acts as having political power before Roman courts and as being a "legal religion" in Rome's eyes, a portrayal that is inconceivable after their disastrous defeat by the Romans in the war of AD 66–70.
- In Acts there is a positive attitude to Roman power that would hardly have been appropriate after Nero's persecution of Christians in AD 65 and beyond. And, significantly, the book ends by affirming that Paul proclaimed the kingdom of God "without hindrance" (*akōlytōs*).
- Specific political and geographical details found in Acts point to a time before AD 72 for its writing (W. M. Ramsay).
- There is no mention of Paul's death in AD 64 or 65 (notice the abrupt ending of the book).

(c) Audience: non-Christian gentiles, represented by Theophilus (Luke 1:3; Acts 1:1).

(d) Place and Circumstances of Writing: Probably Rome; Luke was concerned that "Theophilus" should have reliable information about the beginnings of Christianity (Luke 1:4).

(e) Purposes

- to complete the account of the works and teaching of Jesus, now continued by his representatives empowered by the Holy Spirit (Acts 1:1–2, 5);
- to record the spread of Christianity from Jew to gentile; from Jerusalem the religious center, to Rome, the political center and secular capital of the world (Acts 1:8; cf. Luke 1:1–4);
- to show that Christianity was not a political threat to the Roman Empire, but a "legal religion" (*religio licita*) as the spiritual heir of Old Testament faith (Acts 2:16);

I. INTRODUCTION

- to indicate the rootage of sacred history in secular history (see Acts 11:28 [AD 46]; 18:2 [AD 49]; 18:12 [AD 51–2]; 24:27 [AD 60]).

2. Paul's Letters

   (a) The Extent of the Pauline Corpus

   The majority of scholars acknowledge Paul's authorship of Romans, 1 Corinthians, 2 Corinthians, Galatians, Philippians, 1 Thessalonians, and Philemon. Some question his authorship of 2 Thessalonians, Colossians, and particularly Ephesians. Not a few doubt whether he wrote 1 and 2 Timothy and Titus, commonly known as the Pastoral Epistles. These latter three letters, along with Ephesians, are often referred to as Deutero-Pauline letters, being in their final form produced by Paul's disciples or co-workers but incorporating genuinely Pauline material. The book of Hebrews was associated with the Pauline corpus at an early stage of the New Testament canon, but today it is rarely defended as Pauline. See below (A.2.c).

   We shall be proceeding on the assumption that all thirteen letters mentioned above are authentically Pauline.

   (b) The Grouping of Paul's Letters

   1. Canonical

      Principles of arrangement: (a) churches (A), before individuals (B); (b) according to length (although Galatians is slightly shorter than Ephesians)

      A. – Romans
      – 1 and 2 Corinthians
      – Galatians
      – Ephesians
      – Philippians

3

- Colossians
- 1 and 2 Thessalonians

B. - 1 and 2 Timothy
- Titus
- Philemon

2. Chronological ⟶ 3. Content
(= dominant emphasis)

Galatians	
1 and 2 Thessalonians	Eschatological
1 and 2 Corinthians	
(Galatians?)	Soteriological
Romans	
Colossians	
Philemon	
Ephesians	Christological
Philippians	
1 Timothy	
Titus	Ecclesiological
2 Timothy	

4. Style (Amanuensis)

   A. Gal, 1 and 2 Cor, Rom   Tertius and others (Rom 16:22)

   B. 1 and 2 Thess, Phil, Col, Phlm   ? Timothy (named in each salutation)

When Paul used an amanuensis (Rom 16:22) we have no way of assessing the extent of the scribe's influence, if any, on the language or style of the letter involved. But

I. INTRODUCTION

Paul would always have approved of what was said and how it was said, since the letter carried his name. And we may assume that Tertius would have asked Paul's permission to include his personal greetings. It was Paul's custom to add his personal greeting in his own distinctive hand (Col 4:18; 2 Thess 3:17; cf. Phlm 19).

(c) The Collection of Paul's Letters

There is evidence that even during Paul's lifetime his letters circulated between various churches. His two Corinthian letters were addressed not only to the church of Corinth but also to other believers—"all those everywhere who call on the name of our Lord Jesus Christ" (1 Cor 1:2), or "all God's holy people throughout Achaia" (2 Cor 1:1) as at Cenchreae (Rom 16:1) and Athens (Acts 17:34). Moreover, Paul directed that his letter to Colossae should be exchanged with his letter to the Laodiceans (Col 4:16). Ephesians may have been a circular letter to the gentile churches of Asia Minor (see the textual variants at Eph 1:1), while Romans may have circulated in different recensions of varying lengths (see the textual variants at Rom 15:33). By about AD 65 Peter could refer to "all his [Paul's] letters" (2 Pet 3:15-16).

Regional collections would have grown up spontaneously, both during Paul's life (perhaps at his own initiative; thus D. Trobisch) or after his death (given the high esteem he enjoyed among some of his converts). Some have proposed that Onesimus (Col 4:9) or Luke (2 Tim 4:11) or Timothy (2 Tim 4:9, 13, 21) may have been responsible for an early collection. By the end of the century, about AD 90, several haphazard collections of this kind may have formed the basis of a formal collection.

An initial formal collection may have included **seven** letters (1 and 2 Corinthians, Galatians, Philippians, 1 and 2 Thessalonians, Romans) (thus W. Schmithals); or **ten** letters (the above seven plus Ephesians, Colossians, Philemon) (as reflected in Marcion's *Apostolikon*, about AD 144); or, more probably (on the evidence of allusions in Ignatius and Polycarp), **thirteen** (including the three Pastoral Letters, 1 and 2 Timothy, Titus) (T. Zahn); or even **fourteen** (including Hebrews, through association with a Pauline letter or letters) (C. P. Anderson).

It seems probable that the first collection appeared in codex form (a leaf book of papyrus) rather than on papyrus rolls (J. Finegan). The satirist Martial refers to codex editions of Virgil and Cicero (about AD 85), and T. C. Skeat has argued that the origin of the Christian codex was not later than AD 70. And it appears that from the outset the formal Pauline corpus was a critical text, listing variant readings, following Alexandrian textual techniques (G. Zuntz).

(d) Paul as Writer

The distinction between the "letter" and the "epistle"

More than two hundred years ago the famous New Testament scholar G. A. Deissmann[1] drew attention to the distinction between the "epistle" and the "letter." He regarded the "letter" as:

(i) private, being a confidential, frank, personal document;

(ii) a replacement for face-to-face communication, being a conversation in writing; and

(iii) artless or pre-literary in form, with the author having no intent to publish the letter.

On the other hand, an "epistle," such as Seneca's *De Senectute* ("Concerning Old Age"), is:

(i) designed for the public, even though it be an unknown audience, and so it is an impersonal document;

(ii) non-conversational in diction; and

---

1. For example, in his *Bible Studies*, 2nd ed (Edinburgh: T&T Clark, 1909).

I. INTRODUCTION

(iii) a literary and artistic creation.

Deissmann's distinction is probably overly rigid, reacting as he was to the tendency to treat Paul's letters as "the documents of Paulinism" and as an inspired unity. But in light of Deissmann's basic distinction, we may make two affirmations about Paul as a writer.

First, **Paul was a letter-writer**, in that his letters

(i) are personal and so give a self-portrait;

(ii) show stylistic irregularities that are typical of conversations or dictated letters (e.g., Rom 5:12; 2 Cor 5:6–8);

(iii) are occasional, being prompted by specific circumstances;

(iv) are marked by incidental references, such as personal greetings (e.g., Rom 16:3–16) or asides (e.g., 2 Cor 11:21b, 23a); and

(v) use standard epistolary structure, such as an opening salutation, thanksgiving, and farewell greetings.

Second, **Paul was not simply a letter-writer**, in that his letters

(i) are longer than ancient papyri letters that range from about 20 to about 200 words in length, whereas Paul's letters range from 335 (Philemon) to over 7000 (Romans);

(ii) unlike papyri letters, sometimes mentions co-writers (e.g., the two Thessalonian letters begin "Paul, Silas and Timothy");

(iii) are not private and of passing significance but are marked by lofty themes and intense feelings;

(iv) have a wider audience than friends or acquaintances, since the addressees are fellow believers or spiritual sons and daughters who recognize his authority (e.g., 1 Cor 4:14-15);

(v) are addressed to Christian groups (apart from the Pastorals) and were intended for public reading and sometimes general distribution (see 1 Cor 1:2; Col 4:16; Phlm 1-2); and

(vi) being much longer than papyri letters, can show literary sophistication (e.g., Rom 11:33-36; 1 Cor 13:1-13) and logical precision (e.g., Romans).

3. Relationship of Acts and the Letters

Correlation of Paul's movements described in his letters and Acts.

Letters	Jerusalem Visits	Acts
[Damascus, Gal 1:16-17]		Damascus (9:1-22)
Arabia/Nabatea Gal 1:17)		
Damascus (Gal 1:17; 2 Cor 11:32-33)		Damascus (9:23-25)
Jerusalem (Gal 1:18-20)	1	**Jerusalem** (9:26-29)
		(vision in temple, 22:1-21)
Syria (Gal 1:21)		Caesarea (9:30)
Cilicia (Gal 1:21)		Tarsus (9:30; 11:25)
		Syrian Antioch (11:26)
Jerusalem (Gal 2:1-3, 6-10)	2	**Jerusalem** (11:28-30; 12:25)
Syrian Antioch (Gal 2:11-21)		Syrian Antioch (13:1-4a)
		Seleucia (13:4b)
		Cyprus: Salamis, Paphos (13:4b-12)

I. INTRODUCTION

Letters	Jerusalem Visits	Acts
		Perga (13:13)
Galatia (Gal 4:13)		Pisidian Antioch (13:14–51a)
		Iconium (13:51b; 14:1–5)
		Lystra (14:6–20a)
		Derbe (14:20b–21a)
		Lystra, Iconium, Pisidian Antioch (14:21b–23)
		Pamphylia: Perga (14: 24–26a)
		Syrian Antioch (14:26–28)
	3	**Jerusalem** (15:2–29)
		Syrian Antioch (15:35)
		Syria, Cilicia (15:41)
		Derbe, Lystra (16:1–5)
		Galatic-Phrygia (= Iconium, Pisidian Antioch) (16:6)
		Troas (16:8–10)
Philippi (1 Thess 2:2)		Philippi (16:11–40)
Thessalonica (1 Thess 2:1–2; Phil 4:15–16)		Thessalonica (17:1–9)
		Beroea (17:10–14)
Athens (1 Thess 3:1)		Athens (17:15–34)

9

Letters	Jerusalem Visits	Acts
Corinth (2 Cor 1:19; 11:7-9)		Corinth (18:1-18a)
		Cenchreae (18:18b)
		Ephesus (18:19-21)
		Caesarea (18:22a)
	4	**Jerusalem** (18:22)
		Syrian Antioch (18:22c-23)
		Galatia and Phrygia (= Derbe, Lystra, Iconium, Pisidian Antioch) (18:23)
Ephesus (1 Cor 16:8)		Ephesus (19:1—20:1)
Corinth (2 Cor 2:1; 13:2; cf. 12:14, 21; 13:1)		
Return to Ephesus		
Troas (2 Cor 2:12)		
Macedonia (2 Cor 2:13; 7:5; 8:1-4; 9:2)		Macedonia (20:1b, 2a)
Illyricum (Rom 15:19)		
Corinth (2 Cor 9:4-5; 12:14, 21; 13:1)		Greece (20:2b-3a)
		Philippi (20:3b-6a)
		Troas (20:6b-12)
		Miletus (20:15-38)
		Tyre (21:3b-7a)
		Caesarea (21:8-14)
	5	**Jerusalem** (21:15—23:30; cf. 24:17)
		Caesarea (23:33—26:32)
Rome (Rom 15:23-24, 28-29)		Rome (28:14b-31)

I. INTRODUCTION

B. Suggested Chronology of Paul's Life and Letters

This chronology is from F. F. Bruce, with slight changes and additions (used with permission).[2] Paul's five post-conversion visits to Jerusalem are marked on the right (also see the chart on p. 46).

	AD	
Crucifixion, resurrection, ascension; Pentecost	April–May 30	
Conversion of Saul of Tarsus (Acts 9:1–22; Gal 1:15–17)	33	
Paul's first post-conversion visit to Jerusalem (Acts 9:26–29; Gal 1:18–20)	35	**1**
The ten "silent years"	35–45	
Barnabas fetches Paul from Tarsus to Antioch (Acts 11:25–26)	45	
Famine in Judaea: Barnabas and Paul sent with relief from Syrian Antioch to Jerusalem (Acts 11:28–30; Gal 2:1–3, 6–10)	46	**2**
First missionary journey: Barnabas and Paul visit Cyprus and South Galatia (Acts 13:4—14:26)	47–48	
LETTER TO THE GALATIANS (from Syrian Antioch)	48	
Apostolic Council at Jerusalem (Acts 15:6–29)	49	**3**

---

2. F. F. Bruce, *The Acts of the Apostles: The Greek Text with Introduction and Commentary*, 3rd ed. (Grand Rapids: Eerdmans, 1990) 92–93.

	AD
Second missionary journey: Antioch, Lystra, Derbe, Troas, Philippi, Thessalonica, Beroea, Athens, Corinth, Ephesus, Antioch (Acts 15:36–18:22; 1 Thess 1:2–2:2)	49–52
Paul in Corinth (Acts 18:1–18; 1 Cor 2:1–5)	Fall 50– Spring 52
LETTERS TO THE THESSALONIANS	late 50
Gallio becomes proconsul of Achaia	July 51
Paul's hasty visit to Judea (Jerusalem) and Syria (Acts 18:22)	Spring– Summer 52
Third missionary journey: Antioch, Galatia and Phrygia, Ephesus, Troas, Macedonia, Illyricum, Greece, Philippi (Acts 18:23—21:14)	52–57
Paul at Ephesus (Acts 19:1—20:1)	Fall 52– Spring 56
FIRST LETTER TO THE CORINTHIANS (from Ephesus)	Spring 55
Paul's "sorrowful visit" to Corinth (2 Cor 2:1; 13:2)	Summer or Fall 55
Paul sends Titus to Corinth with the "severe letter" (2 Cor 2:3–4; 7:8, 12)	Spring 56
Paul in Troas (2 Cor 2:12–13)	Spring 56
Paul in Macedonia and Illyricum (Acts 20:1–2; Rom 15:19)	Spring–Summer 56
SECOND LETTER TO THE CORINTHIANS (from Macedonia)	Fall 56
Paul in Greece (Corinth) (Acts 20:2–3)	Winter 56–57

I. INTRODUCTION

	AD
LETTER TO THE ROMANS (from Corinth)	early 57
Paul's arrival and arrest in Jerusalem (Acts 21:17–33)	May 57
Paul detained at Caesarea (Acts 23:33–26:32)	57–59
Paul sails for Italy (Acts 27:1–2)	September 59
Paul in Malta (Acts 28:1–10)	Winter 59–60
Paul arrives in Rome (Acts 28:14–16)	February 60
LETTERS TO COLOSSIANS, PHILEMON, EPHESIANS (from Rome)	60
LETTER TO THE PHILIPPIANS (from Rome)	61
End of Paul's Roman detention (Acts 28:30)	late 61 or early 62
FIRST LETTER TO TIMOTHY (from Macedonia)	63
LETTER TO TITUS (? from Ephesus)	63
Great Fire of Rome; persecution of Christians	64
SECOND LETTER TO TIMOTHY (from Rome)	64
Death of Paul	64–65
Outbreak of Jewish War	September 66
Destruction of Jerusalem	August–September 70

II. LIFE AND LETTERS OF PAUL

WE CAN ISOLATE SEVEN main stages in the apostle's life.
1. From birth to conversion (up to AD 33)
2. Early post-conversion activity (AD 33–46)
3. First missionary journey (AD 47–48) (Acts 13:1—15:35)
4. Second missionary journey (AD 49–52) (Acts 15:36—18:22)
5. Third missionary journey (AD 52–57) (Acts 18:23—21:14)
6. Journey to Rome (AD 57–62) (Acts 21:15—28:31)
7. From his release from house arrest to his death (AD 62–64 or 65).

STAGE I: From Birth to Conversion (up to AD 33)

1. Time of Paul's Birth

(Throughout this treatment of the apostle's life we shall be calling "Saul" by his Greek name "Paul"; only at Acts 13:9 does Luke begin to use this Greek name, "Saul who was also called Paul") (see 2 below).

We have only two indications of Paul's age. One is his self-description in Phlm 9 (written about AD 60): "I prefer to appeal to you (Philemon) on the basis of your love, though I am none other than Paul, an elderly man (*presbytēs*) but now a prisoner for Jesus Christ as well." This key term may be translated "an old man" (NJB, NRSV, NIV, ESV; cf. Luke 1:18; Titus 2:2), "an aged man" = "the aged" (KJV, RV, NASB,

Weymouth), or "an elderly man." The other hint is Luke's mention that the clothes of Stephen's executioners were kept safe "at the feet of a young man (*neanias*) named Saul" (Acts 7:58; cf. 22:20). Traditionally, a *neanias* was a male aged between 24 and 40 (cf. BDAG 667b). In general, a first-century man who survived beyond childbirth and childhood may have lived into his 70s, so we may tentatively suggest that Paul was born at the beginning of the first century AD.

2. Paul's Name and Pedigree

The person we know as the apostle Paul had the Hebrew name of *Sha'ul* after the first king of Israel, transliterated as *Saoul* in Greek (Acts 9:4, 17; 22:7, 13; 26:14) and Grecized as *Saulos* ("Saul") with which the Greek name *Paulos* conveniently rhymes. (Embarrassingly, the Greek adjective *saulos* means "conceited" or "effeminate.") He was born in Tarsus, the celebrated chief city of the Roman province of Cilicia (Acts 21:39; 22:3) in a Jewish family (Phil 3:5) but apparently moved to Jerusalem in his youth ("brought up in this city" = Jerusalem; Acts 22:3) where he undertook advanced study under Rabban ("our teacher") Gamaliel the Elder (Acts 5:34; 22:3), the most renowned teacher of the day and leader of the School of Hillel. Consequently, he conformed to all the Pharisaic traditions (Acts 22:3; 23:6; 26:5; Gal 1:14; Phil 3:6). By birth he was a citizen of both Tarsus (Acts 21:39) and Rome (Acts 16:37–38; 22:25–29). Since he was "born a (Roman) citizen" (Acts 22:28), his father must have held Roman citizenship, possibly as a result of distinctive service to Rome or its representatives. As a Roman citizen Paul had the *cognomen* ("additional name," surname) Paullus. We do not know his *praenomen* ("forename," personal name) or his *nomen gentile* ("family name"). Being a Roman citizen Paul had the right to appeal directly to the emperor (Acts 25:10–11), which had the effect of transferring a case from a provincial magistrate to the supreme tribunal in Rome where the case would be heard by the emperor himself or his deputy.

3. Paul's Persecution of Early Christians

So intense was Paul's opposition to the newly formed and growing group of Jewish apostates who belonged to "the Way" (Acts 9:2; 22:4) that even after the death of Stephen (Acts 7:60) and the expulsion of Hellenistic Jewish believers from Jerusalem (Acts 8:1b), he persisted (note "still" in Acts 9:1) in his systematic arraignment of Christians "from house to house" (Acts 8:3) and "from one synagogue to another" (Acts 26:11). Support for his arrests came from the Jewish Sanhedrin in Jerusalem who provided letters of approval (Acts 9:2; 22:5; 26:10, 12). His persecution targeted both sexes (Acts 9:2, 14; 22:4) and involved efforts to force them to blaspheme (Acts 26:11), threats of synagogue whippings and imprisonment, and even the imposition of the death penalty (Acts 8:3; 9:1; 22:4–5; 26:10). Because Paul says he was personally unknown to the churches of Judea—that must have included Jerusalem—at a later time (Gal 1:22), we must assume that his attacks were directed against the Hellenistic Jewish wing of the infant church that was expelled from Jerusalem and scattered throughout Judea and Samaria (Acts 8:1b).

4. Paul's Conversion and Call

There are three accounts of the conversion of Saul of Tarsus in the book of Acts—one by Luke (Acts 9:1–19) and two by Paul himself (Acts 22:6–11, before the Jerusalem mob in the temple court; and 26:12–18, Paul's apology before Herod Agrippa II). Paul's descriptions supplement Luke's account by providing further details.

- The event occurred "about noon" (22:6; 26:13), with the light from heaven being brighter than the sun (26:13).
- Jesus called himself "the Nazarene" (22:8), spoke in Aramaic, and said, "It hurts you to keep kicking against

the goad" (26:14) ("like an ox kicking against its owner's stick," GNB) (= it is painful for you to keep on resisting the divine call).

- Paul's companions all fell to the ground (26:14), and although they saw the lightning-flash and heard a sound (9:7) they did not understand (*ouk ēkousan*) what the voice was saying (22:9).

- Jesus informed Paul that he appeared to him so that he could be a witness about Christ to both Jew and gentile, bringing them enlightenment and salvation (26:16–18).

The response from heaven to Saul's question "Who are you, Lord?" was "I am Jesus, whom you are persecuting" (Acts 9:5), by which Jesus was totally identifying himself with his persecuted followers (Acts 9:1). This response was probably the genesis of Paul's conviction that the church may be equated with the body of Christ (Col 1:24), a truth dramatically expressed in 1 Cor 12:12 where the word "Christ" stands for the body of Christ: "Just as a body, though one, has many parts, but all its many parts form one body, so it is with Christ." Also, his sight of the glorified Christ may have prompted his description of the "spiritual body" of resurrected believers as glorious (1 Cor 15:43–44; Phil 3:21).

As a result of his conversion, Paul now exhibited in his propagating of the good news about Jesus (Gal 1:23) the same unflagging zeal he had earlier shown in maintaining his ancestral traditions (Gal 1:14; 22:3) and in persecuting the infant church (Acts 9:1-2; 22:4-5; 26:9-11; Gal 1:13; Phil 3:6).

As Paul introduces himself at the outset of his letter to the Romans, the flagship of the Pauline fleet, he begins, "Paul, a slave of Christ Jesus, called to be an apostle" (Rom 1:1). If the surprising word order ("slave . . . apostle"; cf. the similar order in 2 Pet 1:1) is significant, we may safely assume that Paul (and Peter) regarded slavery to Christ as a greater privilege than even apostleship. A slave (*doulos*) is someone whose person and service belongs to another. In Paul's case, that "another" was the exalted Messiah, God's plenipotentiary, whose emissary (*apostolos*) Paul had become in order to preach Christ among the gentiles (Gal 1:10; 2:2, 7, 9). Paul was qualified to be an apostle because of his encounter with the risen Lord (1 Cor 9:1; 15:7–8) and his commissioning by Christ (Acts 26:16–19); while his apostolicity was authenticated by his pastoral fruitfulness (1 Cor 9:1–2), his performance of signs and wonders (Rom 15:18–19; 2 Cor 12:12), and his suffering (1 Cor 4:9–13; 2 Cor 6:4–10; Col 1:24).

STAGE II: Early Post–conversion Activity (AD 33–46)

1. Damascus–Arabia–Damascus (AD 33–35)
   (Acts 9:1–25; Gal 1:17)

   After his disconcerting encounter with Jesus outside Damascus, Paul was led into the city by his traveling companions and began a three-day fast as he reflected on the implications of his revolutionary engagement with the exalted Messiah (Acts 9:7–9). A divinely appointed meeting with Ananias restored his sight and established his calling as God's chosen instrument to proclaim God's name "to the Gentiles . . . and to the people of Israel" (Acts 9:15, 17–18; cf. Gal 1:15–16). After "several days" with his fellow believers in Damascus, he began to preach in the Damascene synagogues, proving that Jesus of Nazareth was the Messiah, the Son of God (Acts 9:19b–22). Then, instead of going to Jerusalem to meet Peter and other leaders in the church there, he went into Arabia and "later" returned to Damascus (Gal 1:16–17).

   In Paul's day "Arabia" may have been a synonym for Nabatea, an expansive area east of the Dead Sea, or it could refer to Arabia Petraea, an area south of Damascus that included both Nabatea and the Sinai Peninsula. We do not know what parts of Arabia Paul visited, and what was his purpose for the visit. It was unlikely simply to have been reflection on the implications of the recent Christophany; his previous three-day fast (Acts 9:9) would have accommodated that need, to some extent. Only some dramatic polarizing action on his part could have necessitated his ignominious departure from Damascus "in a basket from a window in the wall" (2 Cor 11:33) to avoid arrest by the head (*ethnarchēs*, "governor") of a colony of Nabateans in Damascus who represented the Nabatean King Aretas IV (2 Cor 11:32). In all probability it was vigorous Jewish opposition to the apostle's preaching in Nabatea or Arabia that prompted their murderous intent (Acts 9:23-25).

2. Paul's First Post-conversion Visit to Jerusalem (AD 35) (Acts 9:26-30; Gal 1:18-20)

Three years after his conversion (= in the third year after), Paul went to Jerusalem "to get acquainted with Cephas" (= Peter) (NIV) or to interview him (Gal 1:18). In his account of the visit the apostle is stressing his total independence of the Jerusalem leadership with respect to the validity of his calling to preach Christ among the gentiles (Gal 1:16, 18), but he doubtless gained valuable firsthand information from Peter and James about the life and teaching of Jesus during those fifteen days. It is significant that the only two apostles he mentions in 1 Cor 15 as having received a resurrection appearance of Jesus are Peter and James (1 Cor 15:5, 7). At first the Jerusalem disciples were understandably suspicious of Paul's actions and motives (perhaps he was living in his sister's house; cf. Acts 23:16), as they remembered his persistent persecution of their infant church (Acts 9:26). But because of the knowledgeable intervention of Barnabas on his behalf Paul finally enjoyed free movement among his fellow believers and in the city (Acts 9:27-28). But when the local Hellenistic Jews, probably offended by his skillful debating as an apostate, tried to kill him, his friends sent him off to Tarsus via Caesarea (Acts 9:29-30). Further impetus for him to leave Jerusalem came from a vision he received from the Lord while praying in the temple (Acts 22:17–18): "Quick! Leave Jerusalem immediately, because the people here will not accept your testimony about me." But that divine imperative also brought confirmation of his call to the gentiles (Acts 22:21).

3. The Ten "Silent Years" (AD 35–45)

The decade AD 35–45 is called the "silent years" because Luke's record in Acts discloses no information about these years. But Paul himself observes that after his visit to Jerusalem (in AD 35) he went to Syria and Cilicia (Gal 1:21) but was "personally unknown" to the churches of Judea (Gal 1:18–19, 22). These Judean believers had, however, heard of his dramatic conversion and subsequent preaching (Gal 1:22), a report that would have included information about Paul's preaching during some undefined period after AD 35 and possibly included his assumed preaching activity in Syria and Cilicia.

Apart from these implications and assumptions about Paul's whereabouts and actions during this decade, we have detailed knowledge about an event that certainly occurred during these "silent years." In 2 Cor 12:1–10 Paul describes an unforgettable vision and revelation that the Lord Jesus gave him (v. 1). He was caught up into paradise where he was given an inexpressible revelation that no mortal was permitted to repeat (v. 4) and that was stupendously great in nature (v. 7). This experience, during which he was unaware of his bodily state (vv. 2–3), occurred fourteen years before the time of writing (Fall AD 56) (v. 2)—that is, about AD 43 by inclusive reckoning, during these "silent years."

Because Paul wanted to avoid suggesting that this inestimable privilege made him in any sense superior to his fellow believers in status or importance, he objectifies his experience, speaking in the third person about "a man in Christ" (vv. 2–4) and "the man involved" (v. 5). He hastens to note that his heavenly rapture immediately preceded his receipt of a "thorn in the flesh" that God gave him to curb any inordinate pride prompted by the revelation he received in paradise (vv. 6-7). Certainly, Paul's temporary ascent into paradise would have strengthened his resolve patiently to endure his apostolic afflictions (cf. 2 Cor 6:4-10; 11:23-27).

4. Barnabas and Paul at Antioch (AD 45) (Acts 11:25-26)

In Acts 11:25 Luke resumes his account of Paul's movements after he escaped from assassination in Jerusalem by returning to his home city of Tarsus (Acts 9:30): "Barnabas went to Tarsus to look for Saul." During this residence in Tarsus for an undisclosed period, Paul doubtless continued his aggressive evangelism, focusing on the Cilician synagogue there. It was probably at this time that he experienced one or more of the five lashings he endured at the hands of synagogue authorities (2 Cor 11:24). It is possible, too, that in such circumstances Paul was disinherited by his family—as part of his loss of "all things" for Christ's sake (Phil 3:8) (a suggestion of Richard N. Longenecker).[1]

Meanwhile the mixed congregation of Jews and Greeks at Syrian Antioch was flourishing (Acts 11:19-21) and out of concern for its positive welfare the church in Jerusalem appointed Joseph, a Levite from Cyprus, who had the sobriquet Barnabas ("son of encouragement") (Acts 4:36), as their delegate to Antioch. To manage the ongoing revival at Antioch (Acts 11:21, 23-24), Barnabas traveled to Tarsus to invite Paul to join in this flourishing ministry and perhaps give special help with the Antiochene gentiles. Together they taught there "for a whole year" (Acts 11:26). Derisory observers nicknamed this mixed congregation "Christians," that is, "followers of Christ" or "Christ's people" (Acts 11:26b; cf. 26:28; 1 Pet 4:16).

5. Barnabas and Paul Travel to Jerusalem with Famine Relief (AD 46) (Acts 11:27-30)

1. Tremper Longman III, and David E. Garland, eds., *The Expositor's Bible Commentary* (Grand Rapids: Zondervan, 2007) 10:892.

During the year Barnabas and Paul spent ministering in Antioch, a visiting prophet from Jerusalem named Agabus predicted that a devastating famine would spread across the whole Roman Empire (Acts 11:27–28). There is independent testimony of poor harvests and widespread famine during AD 45–47 (e.g., Suetonius, *Life of Claudius* 18.2; Josephus, *Antiquities* 3.320–321). Appointed as emissaries to the churches of Judea, Barnabas and Paul set off for the mother church in Jerusalem with the gift (probably of money and corn) that had been organized in Antioch (Gal 2:1–3, 6–10). If, as is likely, this visit is to be equated with the Jerusalem visit described by Paul himself in Gal 2:1–10, it occurred in AD 46, fourteen years after his conversion in AD 33 (by inclusive reckoning) (Gal 2:1).

Paul met privately with the esteemed (or acknowledged) "pillars" of the Jerusalem church, James, Cephas (= Peter), and John (Gal 2: 2, 6, 9), not seeking their validation of his commission to preach the gospel but desiring their support in exercising that commission, knowing that any cleavage between his mission to the gentiles and the Jewish mission emanating from Jerusalem would totally compromise the overall advance of the gospel (Gal 2:2). At this "famine relief visit" to Jerusalem, three agreements were reached:

- that the gentile mission was legitimate (Gal 2:7–9a);
- that that there was to be an apostolic "division of labor," with Peter's primary emphasis to be on the circumcised (= Jews) and Paul's focus to be on the uncircumcised (= gentiles) (Gal 2:7, 9b); and
- that Paul should go on remembering the poor (Gal 2:10).

With insightful initiative Paul had taken Titus with him to Jerusalem (Gal 2:1), probably as a "test case" or Exhibit A, for Titus was a believer and a gentile and was uncircumcised (Gal 2:3). In spite of pressure from the "no circumcision–no salvation" group at Jerusalem—later identified as "the party of the Pharisees" (Acts 15:5) or as "false believers" (Gal 2:4)—Titus remained uncircumcised. This clearly indicated to the local triumvirate of "pillars" that Paul's gentile gospel was "circumcision free" (Gal 2:3). Verses 4 to 5 of Gal 2 should be regarded as parenthetical: "This issue of circumcision for Gentile believers arose later" (cf. Acts 15:1–29).

6. The "Antioch Incident" (AD 46 or 47) (Gal 2:11–14)

At some stage after the "famine relief visit" (AD 46) to judge by the sequence of events recorded in Gal 2:1–16, but before Paul's first missionary journey (AD 47–48), there was an embarrassing face-to-face confrontation between Paul and Peter at Antioch (Gal 2:11–16).

What caused Paul to believe that Peter "stood condemned (before God)" (Gal 2:11) was Peter's change of attitude and action regarding Jewish–gentile relations (Gal 2:12–13), a change that in Paul's view compromised the distinctiveness of the gospel, namely that through Christ gentiles were justified before God apart from adherence to Jewish law and customs such as circumcision (Gal 2:14, 16; cf. Eph 2:12–16). Peter's about-face that led him to dissociate himself partially from fellow gentile believers, presumably in celebrating the Lord's Supper together and in other ways, was prompted by a desire to minimize antagonism between Judaism and Jewish Christianity and by Judaizers who apparently claimed to be endorsed by James and the Jerusalem church ("certain men from James") (Gal 2:12) and who insisted that only if gentiles followed Jewish customs (Gal 2:14b) and submitted to circumcision could they share in God's salvation. It was Peter's apparent and perhaps temporary concession to this viewpoint under pressure from the "circumcision group" in Jerusalem (Gal 2:12b) that led to Paul's public accusation of hypocrisy (Gal 2:13).

STAGE III: First Missionary Journey (AD 47–48) (Acts 13:1—15:35)

1. Route (see map 1, p. 25)

   Basically, from Syrian Antioch to Syrian Antioch, via Cyprus, Pamphylia, and South Galatia.

   Seleucia–Salamis–Paphos–Perga–Pisidian Antioch–Iconium –Lystra–Derbe–Lystra–Iconium–Pisidian Antioch–Attalia –Seleucia

   In the Mediterranean, travel by sea in merchant ships was deemed too dangerous from September 14 to November 11; thereafter, sea travel was undertaken when weather permitted, but coastal sailing was sometimes undertaken at any time (cf. Vegetius, *De re militari* 4.39).

2. Highlights

(a) Paul's Traveling Companions

   (i) Barnabas

   "Barnabas" was a nickname (meaning "son of encouragement," someone celebrated for encouraging others) given to Joseph, a Levite from Cyprus who was a man of means (Acts 4:36–37). He intervened on Paul's behalf when the Jerusalem leadership were suspicious of Paul's professed conversion (Acts 9:26–27). After ministering with Paul in Antioch for a year, he and Paul were assigned to take the Antiochene relief aid to Jerusalem (Acts 11:22–30). Their next joint appointment by the church of Antioch was to engage in pioneer evangelism in Cyprus and possibly further afield in Pamphylia and Pisidian Antioch (Acts 13:1–14:28). On their third assignment from Antioch, they recounted at the "Jerusalem Council" how the gentile mission had prospered (Acts 15:2–4, 12) and were finally sent back to Antioch with the apostolic letter (Acts 15:22–23, 30–35).

II. LIFE AND LETTERS OF PAUL

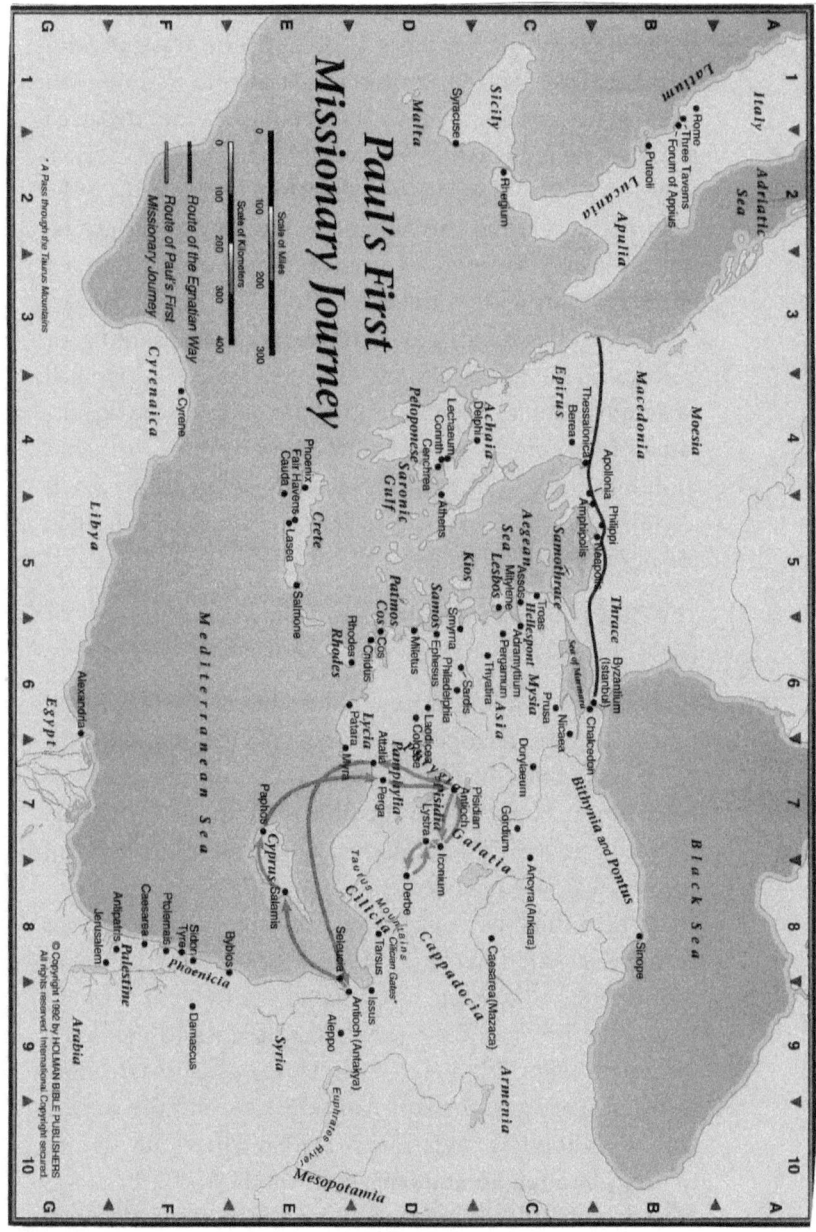

Map 1

(ii) John Mark

Being a cousin of Barnabas (Col 4:10), he traveled with Barnabas and Saul on their evangelism tour from Syrian Antioch to Cyprus as their assistant, but when they departed for Perga he returned to Jerusalem, his home (Acts 12:12), a move that Paul regarded as a defection (Acts 15:38). Why John Mark deserted the mission is unknown. Perhaps he was the supervisor of travel arrangements and the projected change of itinerary to travel inland from Perga to the dangerous Pisidian highlands proved offensive or too daunting, or perhaps he disagreed with the directness of Paul's approach to Sergius Paulus, a gentile. Although Paul decided against taking Mark on his second missionary journey, Barnabas took him back to Cyprus, presumably as his helper (Acts 15:36–39). However, Paul later describes Mark as "helpful to me in my ministry" (2 Tim 4:11; cf. Col 4:10–11; Phlm 24).

(b) The Establishment of a Standard Evangelistic Pattern (Acts 13:5, 14; 14:1; 17:2)

As a Pharisaic Jew and now a follower of the Way, Paul found in the synagogue attendees an ideal audience for his message that in fulfilment of the Scriptures Jesus of Nazareth was the long-awaited Messiah. In the synagogue he could address numerous gentile converts to Judaism (proselytes) and God-fearers along with practicing Jews, all of them suitably prepared for Paul's appeal to the sacred Scriptures (Acts 13:16–41). He had earned a reputation as a distinguished disciple of Gamaliel the Elder and would be invited by one of the synagogue leaders to provide a "word of exhortation" (cf. Heb 13:22) after the reading of the two lessons, the first from the Law and the second from the Prophets (Acts 13:14–15). So when Paul arrived in a city, he attended the synagogue on the Sabbath "as was his custom" and "reasoned with them from the Scriptures" (e.g., Acts 13:5; 14:1; 17:2).

II. LIFE AND LETTERS OF PAUL

(c) The Conversion of Sergius Paulus in Rome-Oriented Paphos (Acts 13:6-12)

Perhaps it was at a banquet given by Sergius Paulus, "an intelligent man" (Acts 13:7) who would be open to new ideas, that Paul met this proconsul. When Luke says that this Roman governor "believed" (Acts 13:12), a genuine conversion to Christ or God is indicated, as is the case when the same verb (*pisteuō*) is used later (Acts 14:1, 23; 17:12, 34; 18:27; 19:18), even though an accompanying baptism is not explicitly mentioned (as it is in Acts 16:33-34; 18:8). Moreover, the magician Elymas had tried (in vain) to turn the proconsul "away from the faith" (Acts 13:8), which would seem to imply "away from believing."

This direct approach to a gentile apart from the synagogue was a parallel to the earlier innovative evangelism of the "men from Cyprus and Cyrene" at Antioch who met with God's approval and blessing (Acts 11:19-21). For Paul, Sergius Paulus's conversion represented a confirmation and vindication of his own calling as apostle to the gentiles.

(d) Paul's Leadership as the "Chief Speaker" (Acts 13:13; 14:12)

Whatever the precise terms of the Antiochene appointment of "Barnabas and Saul" to missionary service (Acts 13:2-3; cf. the earlier 11:26, 30; 12:25; and 13:7), Luke now changes his description of the pair to "Paul and his companions" (Acts 13:13) or "Paul and Barnabas" (Acts 13:42, 46, 50; 14:1, 3), perhaps reflecting the fact that Paul is Luke's hero and was the "chief speaker" in the evangelistic outreach (Acts 14:12; cf. 13:16-41; 14:9).

(e) Ministry in Pisidian Antioch (technically, "Antioch near Pisidia" [Strabo]) (Acts 13:13-48)

Luke's account of the visit of Paul and Barnabas to Pisidian Antioch includes the first of three summaries of Paul's missionary sermons (Acts 13:16–41; cf. the later two précis at Acts 14:15–17; 17:22–31), each reflecting his sensitivity to the audience's background. But this first précis doubtless summarizes his synagogue addresses to a Jew–gentile congregation, with reminders of Israelite history from the Exodus to David's successor, the Savior Jesus, who was crucified and raised from the dead in fulfillment of God's promises, so that forgiveness of sins and justification are granted to all who believe.

Similarly, Paul's preaching in Antioch led to events repeated later—Jewish rejection and persecution (Acts 13:45, 50) that prompted Paul to turn to the gentiles who then believed the word of the Lord (Acts 13:46–48; cf. 14:27; 28:28; Rom 1:16).

3. Aftermath

(a) Demand of "False Believers": "No Circumcision, No Salvation" (Acts 15:1)

At some unspecified time after Paul and Barnabas had reported back to Antioch, "certain individuals came down from Judea to Antioch and were instructing the brothers, 'Unless you are circumcised according to Mosaic custom, you cannot be saved'" (Acts 15:1) (AD 48). These nameless individuals are the "false believers" Paul refers to in Gal 2:4 who secretly infiltrated the ranks of the early believers with their demand, in effect "no circumcision, no salvation." So vigorous was the dispute in Antioch about this issue that the church appointed Paul, Barnabas and others to go to Jerusalem to consult with the apostles and elders (Acts 15:2).

Also in **AD 48** Paul wrote **GALATIANS**, perhaps in preparation for the Jerusalem council of AD 49 (see b below).

Paul's purposes in this letter were twofold.

- To warn the Galatians of their grave danger in following the Judaizers with their "different gospel" (1:6; 4:19–20)

II. LIFE AND LETTERS OF PAUL

and their insistence on circumcision (5:2–3, 6; 6:12–13, 16), a "gospel" that perverts the gospel of Christ (1:7), robs believers of their freedom in Christ (5:1, 13), and reduces them to bondage to the law (4:21– 5:1).

- To urge the Galatians to return to the gospel that they so recently embraced (1:6, 9), a gospel that frees them from legalism (5:1, 13) and that enables believers to live by the Spirit (5:16, 25), to be led by the Spirit (5:18), and to bear the fruit of the Spirit (5;22–23).

(b) The Jerusalem Council (AD 49) (Acts 15:2–29)

The immediate background of the council is described above (a). As Luke summarizes proceedings (Acts 15:4–29), after the Pharisaic party of believers had affirmed their twofold requirement for gentile male believers (circumcision and adherence to Mosaic law) (v. 5), there were three main participants—Peter (vv. 7–11), Barnabas and Paul (v. 12), and James (vv. 13–21)—each in their own way celebrating the spread of the gospel into the gentile world. But in a real sense the whole Jerusalem church was involved (vv. 12, 22).

The outcome of the discussion was incorporated in the council's letter addressed to "the Gentile believers in Antioch, Syria and Cilicia" (v. 23), whose essence is found in vv. 28–29: "It seemed appropriate to the Holy Spirit and to us not to burden you with any requirements beyond these essentials—that you abstain from food sacrificed to idols and from blood and from the meat of strangled animals and from sexual immorality. If you avoid these things, you will do well. Farewell." These three food restrictions and one ethical imperative were designed to facilitate harmonious relations between Jewish and gentile believers and to prevent needless offence to unbelieving Jews in Jerusalem and elsewhere.

So the council successfully dealt with unresolved ambiguities, affirming the legitimacy of the gentile mission and declaring that circumcision and adherence to Mosaic law were not necessary for salvation. Gentile believers did not need to become proselytes to Judaism and attend the synagogue.

STAGE IV: Paul's Second Missionary Journey (AD 49–52) (Acts 15:36—18:22)

1. Route (see map 2, p. 31)

   Basically, from Syrian Antioch to Syrian Antioch, via South Galatia, Mysia, Macedonia, and Achaia

   Syrian Antioch–Tarsus–Derbe–Lystra–Iconium–Pisidian Antioch–Troas–Neapolis–Philippi–Amphipolis–Apollonia–Thessalonica–Berea–Athens–Corinth–Cenchreae–Ephesus–Caesarea–Jerusalem–Syrian Antioch

2. Highlights

(a) One Planned Expedition Becomes Two (Acts 15:36–41)

   Paul's initial plan to revisit churches established in Syria and Cilicia (Acts 15:36, 41) was overridden by a more extensive divine plan when Paul and Barnabas had a "sharp disagreement" over the suitability of Mark as a missionary colleague (Acts 15:37–39a): Barnabas and Mark returned to Cyprus to confirm and expand the gospel inroads there, while Paul chose Silas and set off to strengthen the churches of Syria and Cilicia (Acts 15:39–41).

(b) Paul's Traveling Companions

   (i) Silas

   Silas (= Silvanus of 1 Thess 1:1; 2 Thess 1:1) was a leader in the Jerusalem church, a prophet (Acts 15:22, 32), a Roman citizen (Acts 15:32; 16:37), and apparently a Greek-speaker. He had been entrusted (along with Judas) with the role of explaining and confirming the message of the apostolic letter sent to the gentile believers in Antioch, Syria, and Cilicia (Acts 15:22–23, 27, 32).

II. LIFE AND LETTERS OF PAUL

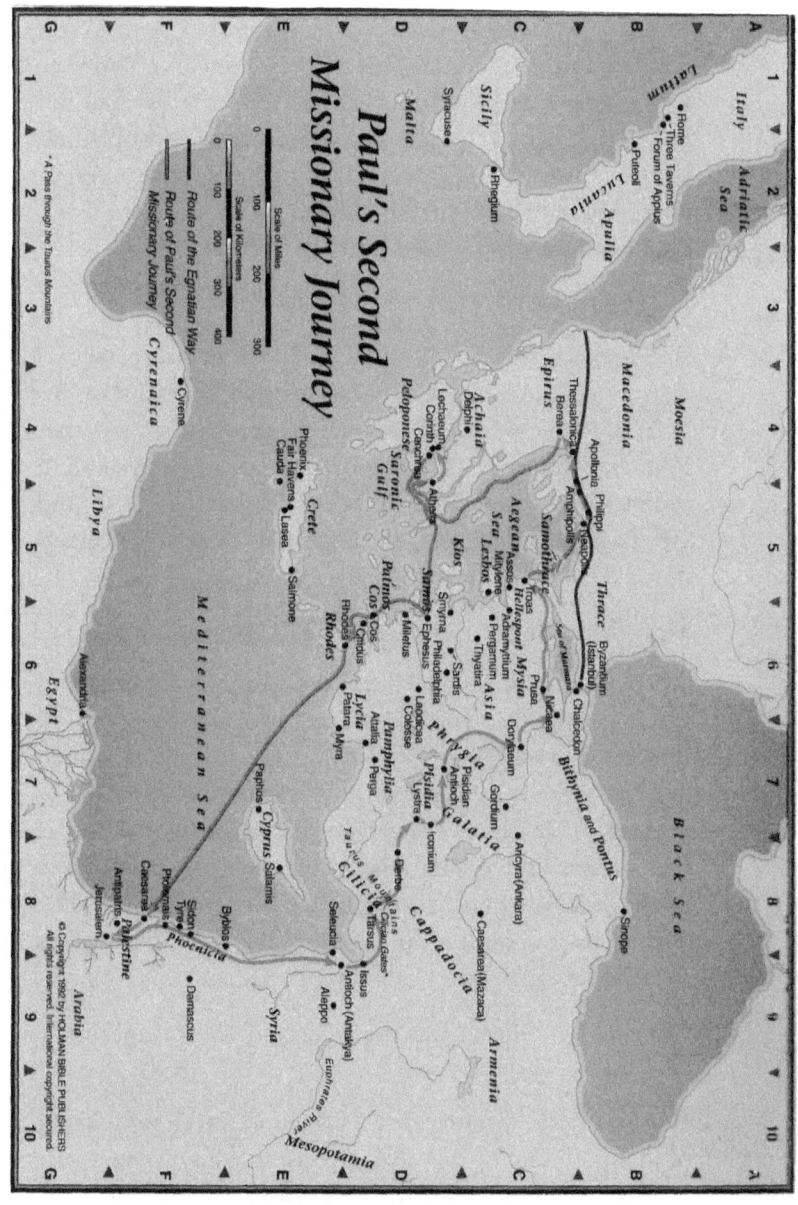

Map 2

(ii) Timothy

Timothy was highly regarded by the believers in Lystra and Iconium, but because his mother, Eunice (2 Tim 1:5), was a Jewess and his father was a Greek and he had not been circumcised, he was not warmly accepted by either the Jewish or the Greek communities. So, wanting to regularize his status and include him in his missionary team, Paul had him circumcised (Acts 16:1-3).

(iii) Luke

Because Acts 16:10-17 is the first of the four "we-passages" in Acts (see I.A.1.a), we may assume that Luke, the author of Acts, has now joined the small group of missionary colleagues from Troas to Philippi. Apparently he stayed on in Philippi when Paul, Silas, and Timothy left, for the second "we-passage" (Acts 20:5-15) begins at Philippi at the end of the third missionary journey.

(c) Movement Westward into Europe (Acts 16:6-12)

After traveling through Phrygian Galatia (= Iconium and Pisidian Antioch), Paul aimed to travel westward toward Ephesus, the leading city of the Roman province of Asia, in keeping with his customary strategic planning. He probably envisaged Ephesus as the center for evangelization around the Aegean. But divine guidance intervened so that the group proceeded north with the aim of entering Bithynia, only again responding to a divine directive and moving westward to Troas and from there to Neapolis and Philippi.

(d) Conversion of Lydia and the Jailer and Their Households (Acts 16:13-34)

Not having the required ten Jewish males who were heads of their households that would constitute a synagogue, the women of Philippi regularly met at a nearby river for worship. One such worshiper was Lydia who had moved from her native Thyatira to Philippi as a dealer in purple cloth.

After she and her household believed and were baptized, she offered hospitality to Paul and his three colleagues (Acts 16:13-15) and her home became a household church (Acts 16:40). Her benevolence as a wealthy woman doubtless formed the pattern for the subsequent generosity of the Philippian church (Phil 4:10-18; cf. 2 Cor 8:1-5; 11:8-9).

Following their exorcism of the slave girl and the attendant riot, Paul and Silas were arrested as disturbers of the peace, flogged, and imprisoned. The earthquake about midnight alarmed the jailer, probably a retired Roman army veteran, who knew his own life would be forfeit if his prisoners escaped. Paul's welcome reassurance that all the prisoners were safe, along with the earthquake itself and the jailer's knowledge of the slave girl's persistent shouting ("These men are slaves of the Most High God, who proclaim to you the way of salvation"), prompted the jailer to inquire about and embrace that way of salvation (Acts 16:16-34).

(e) Strategic Use of Roman Citizenship at Philippi (Acts 16:35-40)

In Roman law it was illegal to punish and imprison a Roman citizen without a trial. Why Paul and Silas did not appeal to their Roman citizenship to avoid the flogging is unclear; perhaps the circumstances of the public uproar and the immediate flogging without the required trial prevented any appeal being heard by the magistrates. Certainly Paul and Silas later ensured that their citizenship was recognized so that the acutely embarrassed and compromised authorities who had acted illegally might afford the infant church protection and even free rein to engage in evangelism after their departure.

(f) Apologetics in Thessalonica (Acts 17:1-9)

Luke does not provide us with a précis of Paul's sermons in the synagogue at Thessalonica but he does afford a precise indication of the content and techniques of Paul's apologetic: his "reasoning" from the Scriptures that involved "explanation" and "proof" (i) that the prophesied Messiah would suffer and then rise from the dead; and (ii) that Jesus was this Messiah (Acts 17:2–3). A similar approach was used in Berea (Acts 17:10–11), Athens (Acts 17:17–18), Corinth (Acts 18:4), and Ephesus (Acts 18:19; 19:8–9). Those at Thessalonica who were persuaded by Paul's "proclamation" and formed the nucleus of a small assembly of Christians included some Jews and "quite a few" wives of leading citizens, but they were mainly "God-fearing Greeks" (Acts 17:4) and other gentiles who turned to God from idols (1 Thess 1:9).

Offended by Paul's direct approach to gentiles and the warm response to his message about Jesus, some jealous Jews engineered a mob riot and laid charges of insurrection against Paul and his new followers before the politarchs (= city officials). Since Paul and Silas were not found in Jason's house, these politarchs required Jason and his friends to post bond, guaranteeing that Paul and Silas would not return (during the tenure of the present politarchs). Paul himself regarded this initiative as a mechanism of Satan (1 Thess 2:18).

(g) Missional Adaptability in Athens (Acts 17:10–34)

Paul was a master of strategic adaptability, witness (for example) his prolonged boasting (with a difference) in 2 Cor 11:16—12:10. Examples of this adaptability at Athens that illustrates his desire to be "all things to all people" (1 Cor 9:22) are multiple.

- In addition to his customary "reasoning from the Scriptures" with both Jews and God-fearing Greeks in the synagogue on Sabbath days, there was daily outdoor evangelism in the *agora* (the marketplace, the center of Athenian life) among any bystanders who would listen (Acts 17:17; cf. 17:2).

- Debating with Epicurean and Stoic philosophers, some of whom ridiculed Paul as someone who retails scraps of secondhand knowledge (*spermologos,* "charlatan," an Athenian slang term), while others more politely imagined Paul was proclaiming new gods, *Jesus* and his consort *Anastasis* (Resurrection) (Acts 17:18).

- Paul's identification of the "Unknown God" whose altar he had discovered during his tour of Athens, as the Supreme God who created everything and superintended human history and who does not inhabit temples made by human design and skill but is close to all humans (Acts 17:22–29).

- Paul cites two well-known maxims from Greek poets—the Cretan poet Epimenides ("In him we live and move and have our being") and the Cilician poet Aratus ("We are his offspring") (Acts 17:28).

- He affirms that the resurrection of Jesus is proof of the coming divine judgment of the world in justice (Acts 17:31).

Although the "Council of Ares" (the Greek god of war), the Areopagus, which exercised jurisdiction in the areas of education, religion, and homicide, apparently failed to grant Paul freedom to propagate his teaching, there was a small but significant response in the city, including Dionysius, a member of the Areopagus (Acts 17:34).

(h) Eighteen or More Months in Corinth (Acts 18:1–18a)

- Paul labored alongside Aquila and Priscilla (= Prisca) in their leatherworking (including tent-making) business and lived with them (Acts 18:3). This couple had recently arrived from Italy because of the Emperor Claudius's edict of AD 49 that all Jews must leave Rome (Acts 18:2).

- After the arrival of Silas and Timothy from Macedonia (Acts 18:5) carrying a monetary gift for Paul (2 Cor 11:9; Phil 4:16), Paul was able to devote all his time to preaching, only to find vigorous and abusive Jewish opposition—that led to divine reassurance (Acts 18:5–6, 9–10). This hostility prompted him to focus his evangelistic effort on gentiles apart from the synagogue, with the result that the house of Titius Justus, a God-fearing gentile, apparently became the site of the first house church in Corinth for believers such as Crispus and his entire household (Acts 18:6b–8).

- Opposition to Paul climaxed when the Corinthian Jews forcibly brought Paul into the marketplace and laid charges against him at the tribunal of Gallio, the proconsul of Achaia. This Roman administrator refused to adjudicate the case since it involved, he said, merely questions about words and names and interpretations of Jewish law (Acts 18:12–15).

This verdict of Gallio, a friend of the Emperor Claudius, implicitly granted Christians recognition as participants in a "legal religion" (*religio licita*) or at least in local "permitted associations" (*collegia licita*), since they were viewed by the Romans as a Jewish sect. The Corinthian church and Christians elsewhere could now assume Roman protection from Jewish interference.[2]

3. Aftermath

There were three consequences of the relative brevity of Paul's visit to Thessalonica (but not simply two to three weeks, as Acts 17:2 might suggest; see 1 Thess 1:9; 2:9; 3:4; 2 Thess 3:8) and his sudden expulsion from the city (Acts 17:2, 10a; 1 Thess 2:2b):

---

2. See further M. J. Harris, *Renowned—But: The Church of Corinth in the First Century AD and Its Relevance for the Twenty-First-Century Church* (Eugene, OR: Cascade, 2022) 9–11.

(i) his longing to see the Thessalonian believers again (1 Thess 3:10–11);

(ii) his frustration at his inability to return (1 Thess 2:17–18) and at the lack of news (1 Thess 3:1–5); and

(iii) insufficient instruction had been given to the new converts (1 Thess 3:10b; 4:13).

Both Thessalonian letters (**late AD 50**) were written from Corinth (see 1 Thess 1:1; 2 Thess 1:1 compared with Acts 18:5). **FIRST THESSALONIANS** seems to have had three main aims:

- to respond to Timothy's encouraging report (and even a letter he may have brought from the Thessalonians) by thanking God for the Thessalonians' stalwart faith and perseverance in the midst of severe suffering (1:2–8; 2:13–14; 3:1–3, 5–7);

- to counter false rumors that Paul had acted from impure motives and had used trickery, flattery, and deceit in his relations with the church (2:3–12); and

- to encourage the believers to continue to please God by personal holiness and mutual love (4:1–12), to comfort them about their deceased fellow believers (4:13–18), and to instruct them about the day of the Lord and appropriate Christian conduct (5:1–22).

Some time later at **the end of AD 50** is also the probable date of **2 THESSALONIANS**. Paul's purpose in this letter was

- to reassure the Thessalonian believers that their patient endurance of persecution and their burgeoning faith and love would be amply rewarded at the spectacular arrival of the Lord Jesus (1:3–12);

- to counter premature excitement about the end caused by pseudo-Pauline teaching, by reminding them of his prior instruction concerning the premonitory signs of the arrival of the day of the Lord (2:1–12); and

- to re-establish orderly balance in the church by sharply reproving some believers who were idle and disruptive (3:6–15).

STAGE V: Third Missionary Journey (AD 52–57) (Acts 18:23—21:14)

1. Route (see map 3, p. 39)

   Basically, from Syrian Antioch to Jerusalem, via South Galatia, Asia, Macedonia, Greece, Asia, and Phoenicia.

   Syrian Antioch–Tarsus–Derbe–Lystra–Iconium–Pisidian Antioch–Ephesus (–Corinth–Ephesus)–Troas–Philippi–Thessalonica–Berea–Corinth–Philippi–Troas–Assos–Mitylene–Samos–Miletus–Cos–Rhodes–Patara–Tyre–Ptolemais–Caesarea–Jerusalem. The bracketed journey (–Corinth–Ephesus), the "painful visit" (see f below), is not included on the map.

2. Highlights

(a) Paul's Traveling Companions

   (i) Timothy (see above IV.2.b.ii) served at this time as Paul's emissary to Corinth (1 Cor 4:17; 16:10–11) and was sent with Erastus from Ephesus to Macedonia (Acts 19:22).

   (ii) In the second "we-passage" (Acts 20:5–15) Luke travels with Paul from Philippi to Miletus (also see above IV.2.b.iii).

   (iii) Gaius and Aristarchus (cf. Acts 27:2; Col 4:10) were seized by the riotous mob in Ephesus and dragged into the theater (Acts 19:29).

II. LIFE AND LETTERS OF PAUL

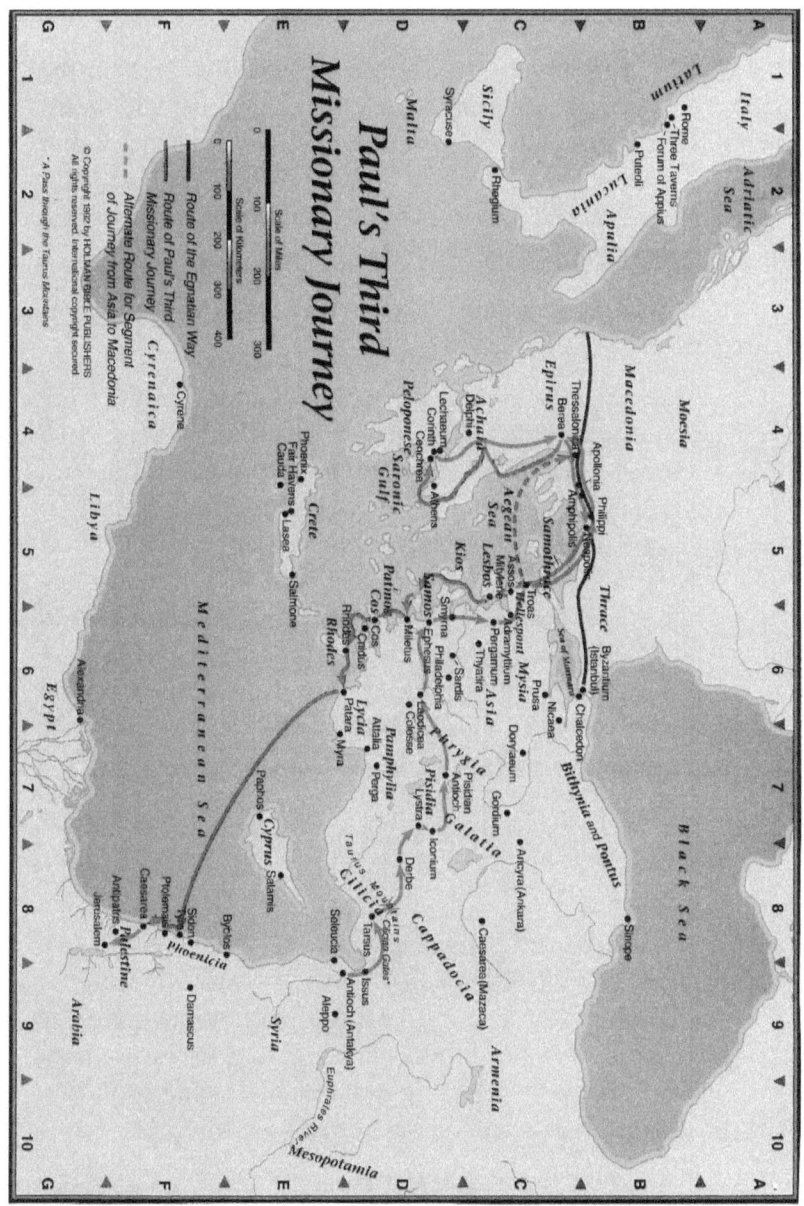

Map 3

(b) Christian Baptism of John the Baptist's Disciples (Acts 19:1-7)

Although the dozen self-described disciples of John the Baptist had been baptized in John's name, when they heard from Paul about John's Successor, Jesus, they believed and were baptized again, this time in the name of the Lord Jesus. After Paul had placed his hands on them, they received the Spirit and exercised the gifts of glossolalia and prophecy.

(c) Discussions in the Lecture Hall of Tyrannus (Acts 19:8-10)

After three months of "persuasive argument" in the synagogue, some unspecified people publicly maligned Paul's message, forcing him to leave the synagogue and for two years use the facilities of the lecture hall of Tyrannus for his public debate. At this point (Acts 19:9) the Western text reflects a probably accurate tradition when it notes that these public discussions continued "from the fifth hour to the ninth," that is, from 11 a.m. until 4 p.m., when most people were resting. During this two-year period Paul himself may have pursued his tent-making during the early morning and perhaps in the evening (see Acts 20:34-35; 2 Thess 3:7-8).

(d) Paul sends his "previous letter" (1 Cor 5:9-10) to the Corinthians

In this letter he directed his converts "not to associate indiscriminately with sexually immoral people." This call for discrimination in social relations was misinterpreted by some to mean that he was calling for total separation from the world. Not so, he now explains; that would require an impossible total withdrawal from the world.

(e) Disclosure and Conflagration as Proof of Genuine Repentance (Acts 19:13-20)

II. LIFE AND LETTERS OF PAUL

As a consequence of the dramatic failure of "the seven sons of Sceva" to exorcise a demon by invoking the name of the Lord Jesus and the painful aftermath (Acts 19:13–16), Ephesian Jews and Greeks were awestruck, "the name of the Lord Jesus was held in high esteem," and many practitioners of magic were converted and openly divulged their magical spells. Moreover, some of these converts collected and burned their magical papyrus scrolls "in the sight of everyone"—scrolls valued at fifty thousand silver coins.

At a time represented by Acts 19:20 ("the word of the Lord spread widely and grew in power") Paul wrote 1 **CORINTHIANS (Spring AD 55)** with three purposes:

- to reply (in chs. 7–16) to a letter delivered to him by three delegates of the Corinthian church (16:17), that raised questions (indicated by "Now concerning . . .") about marriage and celibacy (7:1, 25), food offered to idols (8:1), gifts of the Holy Spirit (12:1), the collection for the poor in Jerusalem (16:1), and the travel plans of Apollos (16:12);

- to express his deep concern over divisions within the church (chs. 1–4), the blatant immorality (5:1–13; 6:12–20), and the improper litigation (6:1–11); and

- to indicate the travel plans of Apollos (16:12) and himself (16:5–9).

(f) Paul's "Painful Visit" to Corinth (Summer or Fall AD 55)

On receiving adverse news about a deteriorating situation at Corinth, Paul seems to have hurried there to reinforce his directive about ejecting the incestuous man from the congregation (1 Cor 5:2, 5, 13) and to forestall any further undermining of his authority by an anti-Pauline clique of intruders from Judea (the "false apostles" of 2 Cor 11:13–15). He describes this brief visit (Ephesus–Corinth–Ephesus) (2 Cor 13:2) as "painful" (2 Cor 2:1; 12:21).

(g) The Demetrius Riot (Acts 19:23–41)

With the success of Paul's evangelism in Ephesus (Acts 19:9–10, 20), there were fewer worshipers of the great goddess Artemis (Acts 19:34) and accordingly a loss of revenue for the city's silversmiths who sold silver miniature statuettes of Artemis. Demetrius, the guild's president, rallied all the relevant craftsmen, and their outrage prompted a prolonged pro-Artemis demonstration in the massive theater, until the influential city secretary or chief executive officer succeeded in quelling the riotous crowd. For the apologetic historian Luke (and Paul) the whole episode provided further evidence that Christianity was no threat to the Roman Empire—there was now not only Gallio's judgment (see above IV.2.h) but also the fact that some of the Asiarchs (provincial officials) of Ephesus (Acts 19:31) whose role was to promote loyalty to Rome, as well as the city secretary (Acts 19:35–41), had intervened on Paul's behalf.

(h) Paul's Distress in Troas and Macedonia (Spring AD 56) (2 Cor 2:12–13; 7:5–6)

Shortly after the Demetrius riot Paul left Ephesus and set off for Troas where he found an open door for evangelism, but he suffered such restlessness of spirit that he was unable to grasp this divinely provided opportunity (2 Cor 2:12–13). So he departed for Macedonia where his deep unease continued as he struggled with internal fears and depression (2 Cor 7:5–6) brought about by the ominous non-arrival of Titus in either Troas or Macedonia with news of the Corinthian reaction to his "severe letter" (2 Cor 2:3–4, 9; 7:8, 12). This letter had called for the discipline of "the one who committed the offence" (2 Cor 7:12) that was probably the public defamation of Paul or his representative. Paul may now have wondered whether his apostolic vocation was in jeopardy.

II. LIFE AND LETTERS OF PAUL

(i) Paul's "Affliction in Asia" (Spring AD 56) (see below, after Stage VII, "Four Low Points in Paul's Career," no. 1)

(j) Visit to Illyricum (Rom 15:19–21)

When Paul states that "from Jerusalem all the way around to Illyricum I have fully proclaimed the gospel of Christ" (Rom 15:19), the phrase "to Illyricum" is inclusive and geographical in sense (not exclusive and metaphorical, "to the far west"). Illyricum (whose southern district is Dalmatia) is the Latin name for the Roman imperial province bordering on the eastern side of the Adriatic Sea, part of "the regions beyond you (Corinthians)" (2 Cor 10:16). This foray into Illyricum represented a new stage in Paul's pioneering ministry (Rom 15:20)—Asia Minor, the Aegean, Illyricum, Rome (and Spain, in intent) (Rom 15:23–24, 28). By this fresh outreach (about which we have no details) Paul was gaining exposure to a foreign Latin-speaking environment, as a prelude to Latin-speaking Spain.

During his pastoral and evangelistic work in Macedonia and pioneer evangelism in Illyricum (see j above) (Acts 20:1b–2a), Paul wrote 2 **CORINTHIANS (Fall AD 56)**, probably in stages. Again, he had three main purposes:

- to express to his friends at Corinth his monumental relief at their positive response to his "severe letter" that had been delivered and reinforced by his emissary, Titus (2:6, 9, 12–14; 7:5–16);

- to encourage them to bring to completion their promised collection for the poor among the believers in Jerusalem before his arrival (8:6–7, 10–11; 9:3–5); and

- to prepare them for his imminent visit by directing them to engage in self-examination and self-judgment (12:14; 13:1, 5, 11) so that they could ascertain the proper criteria for distinguishing between rival apostolates (chs. 10–13) and so that Paul could avoid having to

43

exercise discipline on his next visit (10:2, 5–6, 11; 11:3; 12:19–21; 13:10).

During the three months Paul spent in Greece (= Corinth) (Acts 20:2b–3a) he dictated **ROMANS (early AD 57)** to his amanuensis, Tertius (Rom 16:22). In this letter he hoped:

- to prepare the Roman Christians for his intended coming (1:10–13, 15) by providing them with a comprehensive summary of the gospel that is offered "first to the Jew, then to the Gentile" (Rom 1:16), reflecting his controversies with Judaizers and antinomians (chs. 1–13);
- to warn the "strong" against criticizing or disregarding the "weak" (14:1–15:7) and the whole church against dissensions and heterodoxy (16:17–18);
- to solicit prayer for the satisfactory conclusion of the collection and for deliverance from "unbelievers in Judea" (15:31); and
- to arouse their interest in and support for his proposed Spanish mission (15:23–29).

(k) Delegates for the "Collection for the Poor" (Acts 20:4)

This verse lists the names of the delegates from the predominately gentile churches Paul had established who were traveling with him to Jerusalem to deliver the offering for "the poor" among the believers there (Rom 15:26; Gal 2:10). They were Sopater from Berea, Aristarchus and Secundus from Thessalonica, Gaius from Derbe, Timothy from Lystra, and Tychicus and Trophimus from Asia. No representative from Corinth is mentioned although we know the believers in Achaia also contributed to the collection (Rom 15:26). And Luke may have represented Philippi (note "us" in v. 5).

Among Paul's many motives for organizing this collection during the years AD 52–57 are the following: (i) to express tangibly the interdependence of the members of the body of Christ (1 Cor 12:25–26) in a way that would honor Christ (2 Cor 8:19) and help to effect equality of provision (2 Cor 8:13–15); (ii) to symbolize the unity of Jew and gentile in Christ (Eph 2:11–22) and hopefully win over those Jewish Christians who were still suspicious of Paul's gentile mission; (iii) to dramatize for gentile believers in material terms their spiritual indebtedness to the church at Jerusalem (Rom 15:19, 27).

(l) Raising of Eutychus at Troas (Acts 20:6–12)

Among those present for a celebration of the Lord's Supper in Troas was a young man named Eutychus who was sitting on the ledge of an open window in the crowded room where the smoke of the lamps was having a soporific effect. As Paul continued to talk until midnight, Eutychus dropped off to sleep, overbalanced, and fell from the third floor to the courtyard below and was picked up dead. Paul immediately went down, threw himself on Eutychus, and embraced him, no doubt at the same time praying fervently. His prayer and action brought Eutychus back to life. To the alarmed spectators he said, "Stop making such a hubbub!" After the Lord's Supper concluded, the young man was taken home alive.

(m) Paul's Farewell Speech to the Ephesian Elders at Miletus (Acts 20:13–38)

In this speech Paul highlights several aspects of his three-year ministry in Ephesus (v. 31)—that in spite of vigorous Jewish opposition (cf. 1 Cor 15:32; 16:9) he had declared to both Jew and Greek the need for repentance toward God and faith in Jesus (vv. 19, 21, 24); that he had regularly instructed believers regarding all areas of God's will both publicly and from house to house (vv. 20, 26–27, 31); that he had supported himself, his companions, and others by his own hard physical work (vv. 33–35); and that with his imminent departure for Jerusalem and the advent of ravaging wolves among God's flock, the elders must exercise their shepherding oversight of this flock with all diligence (vv. 22, 28–31).

(n) To Jerusalem via Tyre and Caesarea (Acts 21:1–14)

On his way to Jerusalem Paul spent seven days in Troas and "a number of days" in Caesarea (Acts 21:3, 10). In each case the believers had apparently been informed by the Spirit that hardship and persecution lay ahead for Paul in Jerusalem (cf. Acts 21:10–11), so they tried valiantly to dissuade him from continuing on, wanting to spare him further suffering. But he had twice been directed by the Spirit to go to Jerusalem (Acts 19:21; 20:22) so their pleas were unsuccessful (Acts 20:13–14). A distinction must be drawn between the Spirit-inspired prophecy the believers had received and their natural exhortation based on it. So Acts 21:4b should be rendered "While under the inspiration of the Spirit (*tou dia pneumatos*), they urged Paul not to go on to Jerusalem."

(o) Paul's Five Post-conversion Visits to Jerusalem

	Place of Departure	Date	Acts	Parallels	Purpose
1	Damascus (Acts 9:22–26a)	AD 35	9:26–29	Gal 1:18–20	To interview Peter
2	Syrian Antioch (Acts 11:27–29)	AD 46	11:28–30; 12:25	Gal 2:1–3, 6–10	To carry relief for "the poor"
					To discuss the gentile mission
3	Syrian Antioch (Acts 14:26; 15:2)	AD 49	15:2–29	—	To discuss how a gentile becomes a Christian
4	Ephesus (Acts 18:19–21)	AD 52	18:22	—	To attend Passover?
					To carry a preliminary gift to Jerusalem?

II. LIFE AND LETTERS OF PAUL

	Place of Departure	Date	Acts	Parallels	Purpose
5	Greece (= Corinth) (Acts 20:2–3)	AD 57	21:15— 23:30	Rom 15:25–31	To deliver the collection for "the poor," in the company of the church delegates

STAGE VI: Journey to Rome (AD 57–62) (Acts 21:15—28:31)

1. Route (see map 4, p. 48)

   Basically, from Jerusalem to Rome via Mediterranean ports.

   Jerusalem–Antipatris–Caesarea–Sidon–Myra–Cnidus–Fair Havens–Malta–Syracuse–Rhegium–Puteoli–Forum of Appius–Three Taverns–Rome. The map does not include the first leg of the journey, from Jerusalem to Sidon.

2. Highlights

(a) Paul's Traveling Companions

   (i) Luke

   We can safely assume that Luke accompanied Paul all the way from Jerusalem to Rome, because after the third "we-passage" (Acts 21:1–18, Miletus to Jerusalem) the fourth and last "we-passage" (Acts 27:1—28:16) covers Caesarea to Rome.

   (ii) Aristarchus, a Macedonian from Thessalonica

   He was with Paul in Ephesus (Acts 19:29) and when Paul set out for Rome (Acts 27:2). He joins Paul in sending greetings from Rome (Col 4:10; Phlm 24; both these letters were probably written from Rome) where he shared the apostle's house arrest (Col 4:10). R. N. Longenecker suggests that when Paul embarked for Rome at Caesarea, Luke and Aristarchus may have been entered on the passenger list as Paul's personal doctor and servant.[3]

   3. Tremper Longman III and David E. Garland, eds., *The Expositor's Bible*

PAUL—HIS LIFE, LETTERS, AND TEACHING

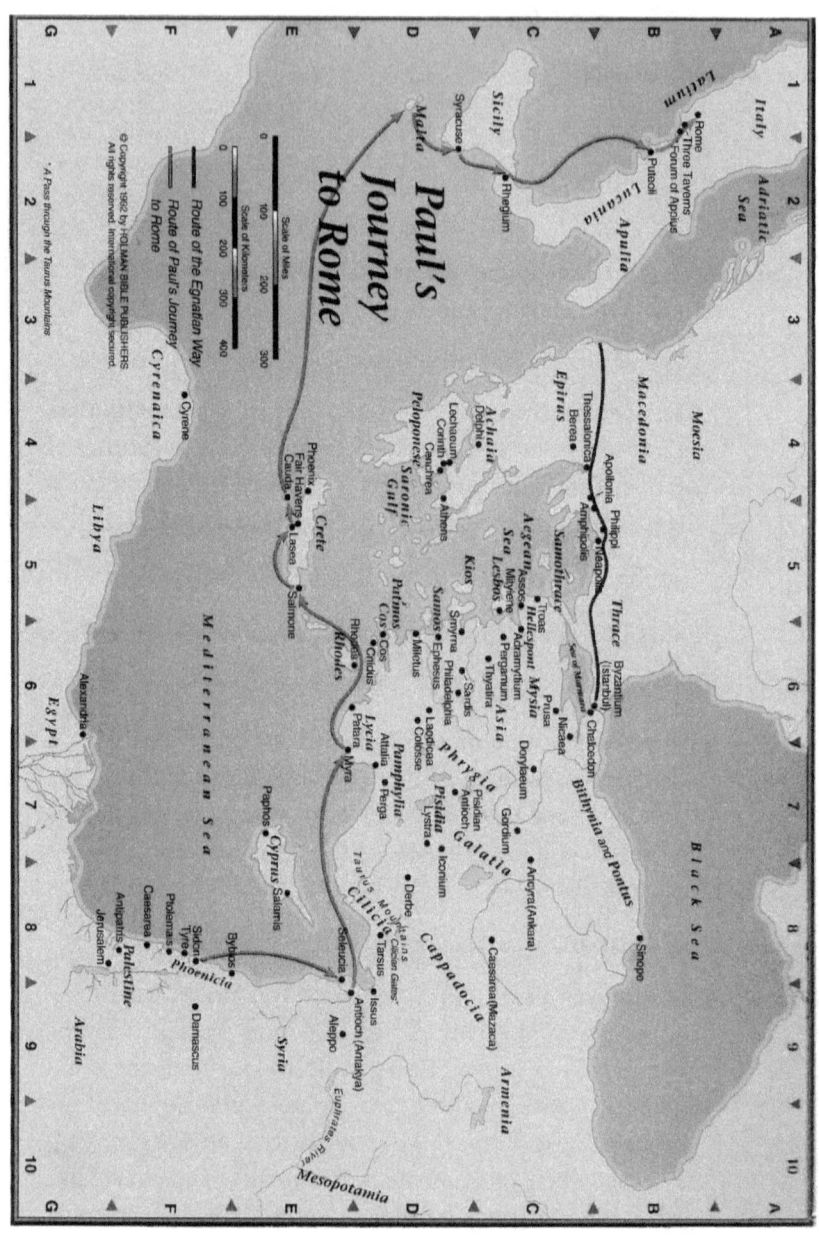

Map 4

II. LIFE AND LETTERS OF PAUL

(b) Purification Ritual in Jerusalem (Acts 21:20-26)

On the arrival in Jerusalem of Paul and the delegates from the gentile churches with the "collection for the poor," the home church (Jerusalem) warmly welcomed them (Acts 21:17; cf. 24:17), thus allaying Paul's fear that this offering might not be favorably received by "the Lord's people there" (Rom 15:31). After reporting the success of his gentile ministry, Paul took four local impoverished Jewish Christians who were under Nazirite vows, joined them in purification rites (coming from abroad, Paul himself was under a seven-day ritual of purification), and paid their necessary temple expenses (Acts 21:26; cf. Paul's own earlier Nazirite vow, 18:18; 19:22). This action was at the strong suggestion of the Jerusalem leaders and sought to prove false a circulating rumor that Paul was teaching Jewish Christians to abandon Mosaic law and not circumcise their children or follow Jewish customs (Acts 21:20-21).

(c) Defense before the Jerusalem Crowd (Acts 21:37—22:22)

When the seven days of Paul's purification were nearly over, some Asian Jews who had come to Jerusalem to celebrate the festival of Pentecost aroused a Jerusalem crowd, claiming that Paul's teaching was offensive to Jews and that he had taken the gentile Trophimus across the balustrade that separates the court of the gentiles from the courts reserved for only Jews. To prevent Paul being beaten to death by the crowd, the commander of the Roman troops (Claudius Lysias, Acts 23:26) in the Fortress of Antonia intervened and arrested Paul who requested and was given permission to address the now silent crowd (Acts 21:27-40).

Although Paul does not respond to the popular charge that he had defiled the temple (Acts 21:28b-29), he focuses on the accusation that he was a Jewish renegade who had abandoned his Jewish heritage (Acts 21:28a). He summarizes

---

Commentary (Grand Rapids: Zondervan, 2007) 10:1083.

his background of birth, upbringing, and education before stressing (i) his unflagging devotion to the Jewish faith as evidenced by his persistent persecution of Jewish apostates, and (ii) the unexpected divine confrontation that prompted his two questions: "Who are you, Lord?" and "What shall I do, Lord?" It was a pious and highly respected Jew, Ananias, who gave Paul the direction he sought, direction later confirmed by a vision in the temple.

There were two different reactions to Paul's defense: the crowd demanded his death when they heard of his divine call to the gentiles, "far away"; the garrison commander arranged for his examination under torture.

(d) Defense before the Sanhedrin (Acts 22:30—23:11)

Still uncertain why Paul's teaching had occasioned such a theatrical response from the Jewish crowd, the Roman commander, realizing how close he had come to committing an offence himself by ordering a Roman citizen to be punished without trial, released Paul and arranged for a special session of the Sanhedrin. At this assembly several events took place in quick succession—Paul's protestation of his innocence, physical retaliation by the high priest, verbal retaliation by Paul, a prompt apology by Paul, his employment of a disruptive strategy by appealing to his hope of the resurrection of the dead, a divisive and then violent dispute between the Pharisees and the Sadducees in the Sanhedrin, and the Roman troops' rescue of Paul (Acts 23:1–10).

After these explosive events, the apostle would have felt dejected: he doubtless recalled the dramatically different demeanor of Jesus and Stephen before this same Sanhedrin, and he now doubted whether his long-standing desire to visit Rome would ever be fulfilled. His precise needs for reassurance were met by the Lord's encouragement the following night, "Keep up your courage! For just as you

II. LIFE AND LETTERS OF PAUL

have testified about me in Jerusalem, so you must testify also in Rome" (Acts 23:11).

This defense before the Sanhedrin gave rise to two episodes involving Paul. First, a plot that was reinforced by an oath was hatched by forty or so frustrated Jews to ambush Paul on the way to a proposed further meeting with the Sanhedrin. But an advance warning to the commander by Paul's nephew foiled the plot. Second, Paul was escorted to Caesarea, the provincial capital, by a massive detachment of infantry soldiers, cavalry, and auxiliaries carrying a letter from Claudius Lysias, the commander, to Antonius Felix, the Roman governor of the province of Judea, summarizing recent events and indicating that accusers had been alerted to be available. Importantly, the letter said, "I discovered that he was accused (by the Jews) concerning controversial questions of their law, but he was charged with nothing deserving death or imprisonment" (Acts 23:29).

(e) Defense before Antonius Felix (Acts 24:1-27)

After Ananias and some Jewish elders had arrived in Caesarea, their lawyer, Tertullus, outlined three charges (one political, one religious, and one legal) against Paul in the presence of Felix (Acts 24:5-6):

- that Paul was a worldwide disturber of the public peace, a creator of political sedition, and so guilty of treason;
- that he was a ringleader of the sect of the Nazarenes; and
- that he attempted to desecrate the temple by taking a gentile inside the barrier.

Paul denied the political charge, claiming that his accusers had no evidence that he argued in the temple or stirred up a crowd anywhere in Jerusalem (vv. 11-13). He partially admits the religious charge, indicating that he still shared Jewish beliefs, although as "a follower of the Way" with its distinctive "people" (vv. 14-17). In vigorously denying the legal issue, he affirms that he was in the temple alone, and ceremonially clean at that (vv. 18–21).

Felix then adjourned proceedings, saying he would decide the case after Lysias Claudius had arrived. But he left Paul in "free custody" for two years (AD 57–59), until he was succeeded by Porcius Festus who was procurator of Judea (AD 60–62) (vv. 22–27).

(f) Defense before Porcius Festus and Paul's "Appeal to Caesar" (Acts 25:1–12)

In spite of pressure from Jerusalem Jews to have Paul transferred back to Jerusalem (so they could assassinate him on the way), Festus held a court hearing in Caesarea at which the Jewish accusations against Paul could again not be substantiated. Once more Paul's defense was "I have committed no crime either against the Jewish law or against the temple or against Caesar" (vv. 1–8). But to curry favor with his Jewish litigants that now included Ishmael the new high priest, Festus inquired about Paul's willingness to be tried before him in Jerusalem. Paul's response was that since no defensible charges had been brought against him, the inconclusive verdict in Caesar's court in Caesarea should stand without a further Jerusalem trial. To break the deadlock, he simply said "I appeal to Caesar" (vv. 9–12). Paul foresaw that one concession by Festus to the Sanhedrin could lead to other more drastic concessions, and that the Sanhedrin would probably exploit Festus's inexperience.

To make this simple appeal, "I appeal to Caesar" (*Caesarem appello* or *ad Caesarem provoco*), was an inalienable right of every Roman citizen. It had the effect of transferring a case from the court of a provincial magistrate to the supreme tribunal in Rome where the case would be heard by the emperor himself or his deputy. Paul was now guaranteed safe passage to Rome. Perhaps he even hoped that a trial before Nero or his deputy might lead to Christians being regarded in Roman law as groups of local "permitted associations" (*collegia licita*).

(g) Defense before Herod Agrippa II (Acts 25:23—26:32)

Festus had been divested of a major problem by Paul's appeal to Caesar but he still needed carefully to formulate the letter that would be sent to the imperial court regarding his prisoner (see 25:26). An unexpected visit of Herod Agrippa II and his sister Bernice to Caesarea to pay their respects provided Festus with a partial solution to this second and minor problem. He reviewed Paul's legal situation for King Agrippa before arranging an opportunity for Paul to restate his defense before a wide audience—a Roman governor of Judea (Festus), a Jewish ruler of the adjoining kingdom to the north (Agrippa II), and "high-ranking military officers and the prominent men" of Caesarea (25:23). Significantly, for Luke's apologetic purposes, the first two declared Paul's innocence (25:25; 26:31–32).

This is the longest of the six Pauline defenses in the latter chapters of Acts. Luke somehow gained legitimate access into the audience chamber of Herod the Great's Caesarean palace to hear proceedings. Here Paul does not address the baseless charges that he earlier faced (Acts 24:5–6) but focuses on the accusation that he was a Jewish apostate.

The defense falls into four parts.

1. (Verses 2–11) As Paul sketches his personal background, he expresses his pride in his Jewish identity as a Pharisee and his faithfulness in preserving the purity of Judaism by the systematic and widespread persecution of all those following Jesus of Nazareth. He argues that he is currently on trial because of his hope, shared by his Jewish ancestors, in a God who raises the dead.

2. (Verses 12–23) After reviewing in detail his transforming conversion experience, he focuses on the

unambiguous directive he received from heaven for him to bring a message of light to both Jews and gentiles by proclaiming the forgiveness of sins through faith in the Messiah whose people he was persecuting.

3. (Verses 24–29) After Festus's high-handed interruption, Paul turns his exclusive attention to Agrippa whom he had already politely addressed directly several times as "King Agrippa" (vv. 2, 7, 13, 19; and the later vv. 26–27). Assuming that Agrippa had an adequate knowledge of Jesus and the Christian movement during the last three decades (26:3, 26), and convinced that knowledge of the Jewish prophets would lead to belief in Jesus as the promised Messiah, Paul asked Agrippa directly, "Do you believe the prophets?" Embarrassed in front of the distinguished audience, the king parodies Paul's question, "Are you trying to persuade me to play the part of a Christian in such a short time?" (Acts 26:28).

4. (Verses 30–32) The verdict of the Big Three at the hearing—Festus, Agrippa, and Bernice—was that nothing Paul was doing deserved death or imprisonment.

(h) Storm and Shipwreck (Acts 27:13–44)

Sailing along the southern coast of Crete in the Adrian Sea, Paul and his fellow shipmates encountered a violent storm, a "northeaster" (NIV), for fourteen days and nights. In spite of undergirding and reinforcing the hull with ropes, throwing the deck cargo of wheat along with the shop's tackle overboard, and dropping four anchors from the stern as a brake, they were unsuccessful in preventing their being shipwrecked on a sandbar, with everyone reaching land either by swimming or by grasping pieces of the wreck.

Paul's natural leadership was evident in several ways. (1) By giving sound advice (not taken at first) he gained the confidence of Julius, the centurion (vv. 21, 43), who with his soldiers was transporting grain to Rome and was responsible for safely escorting prisoners there. (2) He informed the pessimistic sailors of his heavenly vision that only the ship, not its crew and prisoners totalling 276, would be destroyed (vv. 21-26; cf. v. 44). (3) He reported to Julius the sailors' foolish attempt to escape, insisting that the whole crew was needed for everyone to survive (vv. 30-32). (4) He wisely urged everyone to begin eating again so as to gain strength for the effort to reach shore (vv. 33-36).

(i) Reassurances at Malta (Acts 28:1-10)

Paul's stay in Malta for about three months (Acts 28:11) was marked by two events. One revealed divine protection, when he suffered no ill effects from the snake hanging from his hand (vv. 3-6). The other event revealed divine power operating through Paul, as he was enabled to heal the father of Publius, "the chief official of the island," who was suffering from fever and dysentery, and then large numbers of the island's inhabitants (vv. 7-10).

Both events would have reassured Paul of his God-given mission and fortified him for his upcoming stressful Roman imprisonment, after the emotional challenges of two frustrating years in Caesarea and fourteen life-threatening days at sea.

(j) Defense before Jewish Leaders (Acts 28:17-28)

Paul's interaction with the local Jewish leaders in Rome was in two stages. After arriving in Rome he promptly invited a small group and summarized his present situation as an imprisoned Roman citizen awaiting trial before the emperor or his deputy. He was innocent of any charge that he had attacked Jewish people or their customs. In fact the Roman authorities had declared him innocent of any crime deserving death and wanted to release him. He had appealed to Caesar only because of Jewish objection to his innocence (vv. 17-20). In reaction to Paul's assertions, the

Jewish leaders with polite reserve claimed ignorance about Paul and his teaching but expressed a wish to hear more about "this sect" (vv. 21–22).

At the second arranged meeting, where numbers were larger, Paul spoke of theological, not political or legal matters. The messianic hope of Israel, expressed in the Law and the Prophets, was fulfilled in Jesus of Nazareth (v. 23). In the partially negative reaction to his defense, Paul saw a fulfilment of Isa 6:10.

(k) "Free Custody" in Rome (Acts 28:30–31)

As earlier in Caesarea (Acts 24:23), so now in Rome Paul experienced what the Romans called "free custody" (*libera custodia*). He was "in his own rented house" (Acts 28:16, 23, 30), permanently manacled to a soldier (Acts 28:16, 20; note the reference to "chains" in Eph 6:20; Phil 1:7, 13–14, 17; Col 4:18; Phlm 13), but permitted to have friends (such as Epaphras, Phlm 23) visit and attend to personal needs. This was Paul's situation when he wrote his four Captivity Epistles.

COLOSSIANS (AD 60)

While Paul was imprisoned in Rome, he was visited by Epaphras (Col 1:8; Phlm 23) who informed him of the spiritual progress of the Colossian congregation and of two dangers confronting the church. In response to this news, Paul dictated this letter to his amanuensis, aiming (1) to applaud their faith, love, and hope (Col 1:3–8; 2:5), but also (2) to warn them of the danger of relapsing into pagan ways of thinking and acting (3:5–11) and of accepting unorthodox teaching (1:23; 2:1–23).

PHILEMON (AD 60)

Onesimus, a slave of Philemon in Colossae, had not only run away from his master to Rome (vv. 15–16), but also had left with some of Philemon's money or possessions (vv. 18–19). Paul, having led Onesimus to faith in Christ (v. 10), now sends him back to Philemon (v. 12) in the company of Tychicus who is delivering Colossians and Ephesians (Col 4:7–9; Eph 6:21–22). The letter Onesimus carries (viz. Philemon) has two main purposes: to afford Philemon the opportunity to receive Onesimus back as a Christian brother (v. 16) and to release him for further service for Paul (vv. 13–14, 20–21).

EPHESIANS (AD 60)

Whereas all of Paul's other letters were, at least in part, written to address specific needs in specific local congregations, Ephesians is unique in being a circular letter, copied in and distributed from Ephesus, and addressed not only to the Ephesian believers but also to Christian communities in the hinterland of Ephesus. Its purpose is therefore more general—to encourage its readers or hearers to appreciate their elevated heavenly calling and to dramatize it by conduct empowered by the Holy Spirit and benefitting others. Fittingly, then, it has been called "the quintessence of Paulinism" (F. F. Bruce).

PHILIPPIANS (AD 61)

This letter was almost certainly written after the other three Captivity Epistles, toward the end of Paul's two-year detention, since:

- his circumstances and prospects had altered since the time reflected in Acts 28:30–31. "Free custody" "in his own rented house" had given place to confinement, probably in the barracks of the Praetorian Guard (Phil 1:13);

- he observes that "the whole Praetorian (or, palace) Guard" knew that his imprisonment was "for the sake of Christ" (Phil 1:13; cf. 4:22);
- hostility to Paul within some of the local congregations or by itinerant preachers was flourishing (Phil 1:15–18); and
- his trial apparently had begun (Phil 1:7b).

Four purposes seem to lie behind Paul's letter to the Philippians.

1. to encourage them to rejoice in the Lord in spite of their adverse circumstances (2:18; 3:1; 4:4), especially since Paul himself, in prison, was rejoicing in the divine superintendence of his affairs (1:3–26; 2:17–18; 4:10–13);
2. to thank the church for its gift sent by Epaphroditus (4:10–20);
3. to commend Epaphroditus to the Philippians, possibly against the criticism that he was deserting Paul by returning to Philippi (2:25–30); and
4. to promote internal unity among the Philippians (1:27–30; 2:1–5; 4:1–3).

STAGE VII: From Paul's Release from House Arrest to His Death (AD 62–64 or 65)

1. Route: Basically, from Rome to Rome, with undisclosed movements in the eastern Mediterranean, especially the Aegean Sea, and possibly a visit to Spain.
2. Defensible Assumptions: This proposal is based on several defensible assumptions.

    (a) The Pastorals (1 and 2 Timothy and Titus) Were Written by Paul.

All three letters claim to be written by Paul (1 Tim 1:1; 2 Tim 1:1; Titus 1:1). The differences in vocabulary and style between these letters and the undisputed Pauline letters may be largely accounted for by the dramatically different audiences—not struggling infant churches but Paul's trusted delegates commissioned by him to deal with particular pastoral problems and needs. The two main alternatives to Pauline authorship—pseudonymity and the "fragments hypothesis"—create more unresolved difficulties than those prompted by the traditional view.

FIRST TIMOTHY was written probably from Macedonia in **AD 63** with two main purposes: (1) to give Timothy, Paul's deputy, directions regarding congregational issues in churches in and around Ephesus, issues such as false teachers (1:3–7; 4:1–5; 6:2b–10), the conduct of worship (2:1–15), qualifications for leaders (3:1–13), and proper care for widows (5:3–16); (2) to encourage Timothy to exercise his God-given gifts and set an example of pure conduct (4:6–16; 6:11–14).

In **TITUS**, perhaps written from Ephesus, also in **AD 63**, Paul seeks to encourage and admonish Titus in the performance of his pastoral ministry in Crete (1:5). The recurrent theme relates to "what(ever) is good" or "good deeds" (1:8, 16; 2:7; 3:1, 8, 14). Titus was to appoint elders who love "what is good" (1:5–9), to rebuke rebellious people who fail to do "what is good" (1:10–16), and to instruct believers to teach and do "what is good" (2:1–15; 3:1–11, 14).

SECOND TIMOTHY was sent from Rome (see 1:17), probably in **AD 64** (? the date of Paul's death) shortly before his martyrdom (4:6–8). It reads like Paul's "last will and testament," as he focuses on his own present suffering (1:8, 12; 2:3; 4:14–18) and sense of being deserted on many fronts (1:15; 4:9–11, 16). He applauds

Timothy's resilient faith (1:4–5) and exhorts him to persevere as an unashamed worker (2:15; 3:10–17), reminding him that Christian ministry (4:1–5) is like the service rendered by the soldier, athlete, farmer, workman, instrument, and slave (2:1–7, 14–26).

(b) Geographical References Are Accurate: The geographical references in the Pastorals that involve Paul are accurate and focus on the Aegean Sea.

These references are Miletus (2 Tim 4:20), Ephesus and Macedonia (1 Tim 1:3; 3:14–15), Troas (2 Tim 4:13), Philippi (Phil 2:24), and "the province of Asia" (2 Tim 1:15). Elsewhere in the eastern Mediterranean: Nicopolis (Tit 3:12), Crete (Titus 1:5), and Rome (2 Tim 1:16–17).

It is uncertain whether Paul ever fulfilled his desire to visit Latin-speaking Spain with the gospel (Rom 15:24, 28). First Clement 5:6–7, however, speaks of Paul as having "preached in the East and in the West . . . having taught righteousness to the whole world and having reached the extreme West" (? = the Straits of Gibraltar, or the western extremity of Spain). Less probably, the crucial phrase (*to terma tēs dyseōs*) could be rendered "the goal (or, limit) of the West" (= Rome).

(c) Paul Released, Then Later Arrested: Paul was released from his two-year house arrest in Rome (Acts 28:30) but was later arrested, tried, and executed in Rome under Nero (2 Tim 4:6, 16–18).

In letters written during his house arrest, he anticipates his release (Phil 1:25; 2:24; Phlm 22) which seems to have occurred, either because he had been tried and acquitted (see Acts 27:24), or because his case was dismissed since no charge had been laid by the Jerusalem Jews, or because the statutory eighteen-month period for trial had expired.

II. LIFE AND LETTERS OF PAUL

Paul's second detention in Rome differed from the first in that it was more rigorous (2 Tim 2:9) and he anticipated his death (2 Tim 4:6–7). The charge he faced may have been that he was a leader of the despised Christians (see Tacitus, *Annals* 15.44.3–8) and had been the regular instigator of riots in the Roman provinces (cf. Acts 24:5). The trial seems to have been in two stages: first, a preliminary investigation ("at my first defense," 2 Tim 4:16) after which he remained in custody, and then the formal trial itself at which he was found guilty and then executed.

(d) Alternative Views Are Less Convincing: Alternative views about Paul's final days are less convincing explanations of all the relevant data.

- Paul was tried, found guilty, and then suffered a martyr's death at the end of his two-year detention in Rome.
- Paul suffered the punishment of exile (cf. 1 Clem 5:6) after a trial following his two-year detention in Rome.
- Paul experienced a more rigorous confinement after his two-year detention, leading ultimately to his trial and death in Rome.

Paul as a Missionary Statesman

A. To speak of Paul's "missionary strategy" is not to imply that his every move was premeditated and contributed to the execution of some detailed and carefully executed plan. Nor does it, on the other hand, imply his unspirituality, as though he were some scheming and unscrupulous tactician. Rather, to investigate Pauline missionary and pastoral methods is to discover that he was directed and inspired by a God whose *modus operandi* is orderly, not chaotic; methodical, not confused. Yet Paul's planning was not infrequently overridden by circumstances (e.g., Gal 4:13) or by direct divine intervention (e.g., Acts 16:6).

B. Features "normative" for Paul but "non-normative" for other believers

1. His practice of offering the gospel "to the Jew first" (Rom 1:16; cf. Luke 24:47; John 4:22; Acts 2:39).

2. His cultivation of geographical virgin soil (Rom 15:20; cf. 2 Cor 10:13–18).

3. His assumption, where appropriate, of "pre-evangelism" (through instruction given in the synagogues of the dispersion; e.g., Acts 17:1–4).

4. His calling to and preference for an itinerant ministry (thus "Paul the traveler"). Estimates of the total distances Paul traveled vary considerably, but one estimate suggests that during his three missionary journeys and his journey to Rome he traveled (on foot, donkey/horse, or ship) a total of over 5000 miles/8000 kilometers on land and about 5,300 miles/8,500 kilometers by sea.[4]

5. His refusal to receive financial support from any church in which he was currently ministering (2 Cor 11:7–12; Phil 4:15–16).

6. His personal appointment of elders (Acts 14:23; cf. Titus 1:5).

7. His appeal to his apostolic authority (1 Cor 9:1; 2 Cor 10:8; 13:10).

C. Features "normative" for Paul and subsequent believers

1. His concentration on large urban centers (e.g., Acts 17:1, 10, 15), successively Antioch, Corinth, Ephesus, Caesarea, Rome.

2. His establishment of household churches within the city (e.g., Acts 16:40; 18:8; Rom 16:5; 1 Cor 1:16) as the organ for the spread of the gospel (e.g., Rom 16:10–11; 1 Cor 16:15).

---

4. J. Spriggs, "Travel in the Roman Empire during the First Century," *Biblical Archaeological Review* 1 (1985) 1–7.

II. LIFE AND LETTERS OF PAUL

3. His dependence on co-workers (e.g., Rom 16:1–3, 9) and the creation of a spiritual succession by the mentoring of selected colleagues (e.g., 1 Tim 1:2; 3:14; 2 Tim 1:2; 2:2; Titus 1:4–5; 2:1).

4. His preoccupation with preserving the unity of the church (e.g., 1 Cor 1:10–13; Eph 4:3), but not at the expense of accommodating false teaching (e.g., Rom 16:17–18).

5. His sensitivity to the needs of a situation (e.g., Acts 19:37; 24:10–21, 24).

6. His pastoral adaptability (e.g., Acts 16:3 and Gal 2:3; 1 Cor 9:19–23; 2 Cor 1:15–17; 11:16–19).

Four Low Points in Paul's Career

From Paul's own letters (and in one case from Acts 23) we can identify four occasions when he felt alone and discouraged, significantly all occurring in his maturity. There were doubtless other times when (we may surmise) he felt greatly disheartened by his circumstances, such as his stoning at Lystra (Acts 14:19) or his predicament during the storm at sea on his journey to Rome (Acts 27:20, where Luke says "we finally gave up all hope of being saved"; 2 Cor 11:25).

1. In Asia, probably in Spring AD 56 (2 Cor 1:8–11)

In most of his letters addressed to churches Paul follows his salutation with an expression of thanksgiving for his readers—but not so at the beginning of 2 Corinthians, where he is strangely preoccupied with his own situation as he gives thanks to God for his recent deliverance from a devastating "affliction" (*thlipsis*) that he experienced in Asia. The Paul who elsewhere confesses that "nothing is beyond my power in the strength of him who makes me strong" (Phil 4:13 TCNT) now asserts that this affliction was "beyond measure, beyond my capability to cope with, so that we were forced to abandon even any hope of survival" (2 Cor 1:8). So debilitating was the affliction that he felt he had received a death sentence, with the result that the divine deliverance from its ravages was equivalent to a resurrection from the dead (2 Cor 1:9). Moreover, the experience was likely to recur, so he requested the Corinthians' prayerful support (2 Cor 1:10-11).

Various identifications of this affliction have been proposed—opposition to Paul at Ephesus (1 Cor 15:32; 16:9), imprisonment (2 Cor 11:23), his suffering of "the thirty-nine lashes" (2 Cor 11:24), the Demetrius riot (Acts 19:23-41); but most probably it was a prostrating attack of a recurrent malady that he later identifies as a "thorn in my flesh" (2 Cor 12:7-9).[5]

2. In Macedonia in about AD 56 (2 Cor 7:5-7)

Paul had sent Titus, his deputy, to Corinth with a "severe (or, sorrowful) letter" (2 Cor 2:4; 7:8) (no longer extant) that called for the Corinthian believers to repent of their support for those who were opposing Paul. When Titus did not arrive in Troas with news of Corinth, Paul "had no peace of mind" and went on to Macedonia (2 Cor 2:12-13) where his restlessness of spirit continued and he was "harassed in every way—outwardly there were conflicts (*machai*), and inwardly fears (*phoboi*)" (2 Cor 7:5).

What were Paul's multiple fears? Basically, the future of his whole ministry at Corinth and elsewhere was at stake. But more specifically, in his present situation there was a haunting uncertainty about Titus's reception at Corinth (cf. 2 Cor 7:13, 15); a persistent apprehension about the Corinthian reaction to the "severe letter" delivered by Titus, especially given Titus's failure to meet Paul at Troas as planned (2 Cor 2:13) and initially in Macedonia (2 Cor

---

5. For a discussion of the nature and significance of Paul's "affliction in Asia" and his "thorn in the flesh," see M. J. Harris, *The Second Epistle to the Corinthians: A Commentary on the Greek Text* (Eerdmans: Grand Rapids, 2005) 164-82, 851-61.

7:5); anxiety that he had caused the Corinthians unnecessary pain by his "severe letter" (cf. 2 Cor 7:8) with its call for disciplinary action against the wrongdoer (cf. 2 Cor 2:6–7); concern that his boasting to Titus about the Corinthians might prove unfounded and therefore acutely embarrassing (cf. 2 Cor 7:14); anxiety about the safety of Titus in travel; apprehension that on his forthcoming visit to Corinth he might find some members indulging in unchristian conduct (2 Cor 12:20–21).

Relief came to Paul in his downcast, anxious state only by the safe arrival of Titus with favorable news of the Corinthians' positive response to the "severe letter" (2 Cor 7:6–13). "God, the Comforter of the depressed (*tous tapeinous*), comforted us" (= me, who was depressed, by implication) (v. 6). When the adjective *tapeinos* is used of an emotional state, it means "downcast" or "dejected" or "disheartened" or "depressed." With Titus's arrival and his news about Corinth, Paul's dejection gave way to consummate relief and deep joy (2 Cor 7:8–13).

3. In Jerusalem in about AD 57 (Acts 23:1–11)

Shortly after Paul's arrival in Jerusalem, Asian Jews prompted a popular uprising against Paul that led the Roman military commander to arrest Paul and finally have him address the summoned Jewish Sanhedrin. Paul unwisely began his defense with a vigorous assertion of his innocence before God (v. 1). When the high priest Ananias illegally ordered Paul to be struck, the apostle, who had not been charged, let alone found guilty, lashed out verbally, "God will strike you, you whitewashed wall!" But then, just as abruptly, he apologized for his ill-considered outburst (vv. 3–5). Then he engineered a stratagem that effectively divided the Sanhedrin but prompted a violent dispute that endangered his own life (vv. 6–10).

After all this Paul was undoubtedly despondent as he sat alone in his cell in the Fortress of Antonia. (1) When he recalled the calm demeanor of Jesus and Stephen before the same Sanhedrin (Matt 26:59–63; Acts 6:15; 7:54–56, 59–60), he must have felt saddened by his own dismal performance in the same arena. (2) He had put his own life in danger by his divisive maneuver (Acts 23:10). (3) He now doubted whether his long-standing desire, as a Roman citizen (Acts 22:27) and Christian, to visit Rome would be fulfilled.

These precise concerns were graciously addressed by the risen Jesus. "The following night the Lord stood near Paul and said, 'Take courage! As you have testified about me in Jerusalem (Acts 22:1–21; 23:6), so you must also testify in Rome'" (v. 11).

4. In Rome in about AD 64 (2 Tim 4:9–18)

   For the second time in his career Paul is in Rome under guard (for the earlier occasion, see Acts 28:16, 30–31). But this time there are differences: he is awaiting a final trial but anticipates legal delays that will permit visits from his colleagues (2 Tim 4:9, 11, 13, 16, 21); he is not making plans for travel after his release (compare Phlm 22) but expects conviction after his trial and death as a martyr (2 Tim 4:6–8).

   What hints are there in the text that he is grappling with loneliness, frustration, and despondency?

   - His immediate circle of colleagues had broken up—Demas had gone to Thessalonica, Crescens to Galatia, Titus to Dalmatia, and he had sent Tychicus to Ephesus (vv. 10, 12).
   - Demas, his onetime co-worker (Col 4:14; Phlm 24), had deserted Paul because of his "love of the present world" (2 Tim 4:10)—perhaps departure from the faith, perhaps unwillingness to face martyrdom with Paul.

- His request that Timothy should join him "quickly," because of Demas's desertion (vv. 9–10; cf. vv. 11, 21).
- After his first defense, probably a preliminary investigation of his case prior to his formal trial, there was no support of any kind from the local Roman believers, a serious sin of omission ("May it not be counted against them!") (v. 16).
- Twice Paul uses a colorful verb to depict his sense of being let down (vv. 10, 16). In derivation *egkataleipō* denotes the complete (*kata*) desertion (*leipō*) of someone who is in the midst of (*en*) a situation where aid is urgently needed. Paul had felt abandoned, "left in the lurch." Like Jesus who was abandoned by his disciples in his hour of need (Mark 14:50), Paul felt forsaken by those who ought to have stood with him (cf. 1:15).

But, once again, the Lord Jesus stood by his side and gave him strength (v. 17; cf. Acts 18:9–10; 22:17–21; 23:11).

In the first, third, and fourth instances mentioned above, God the Father or the Lord Jesus intervened directly to bring the needed comfort and strength, while in the second case the divine comfort was mediated through Titus.

III. TEACHING OF PAUL

A. Sources of Paul's Teaching

1. Old Testament

   The origin of Paul's fundamental and formative theological concepts is not to be found primarily in Hellenism but basically in the Old Testament (which he cites ninety-three times), as reflected in his training in rabbinic Judaism. See 2 Cor 11:22; Gal 1:14; Phil 3:5-6.

2. Hellenism

   No rigid distinction can be drawn between diaspora and Palestinian Judaism; there was rich cross-fertilization between the two in the first century. Although his formal academic training was in Jerusalem (Acts 22:3; 26:4) (see above I.C.1)., he was born in Tarsus of Cilicia, and for a decade (AD 35-45) before his first missionary journey he moved in a Hellenistic atmosphere (Syria and Cilicia). Notable also is his use of the Septuagint (fifty-one of his ninety-three OT citations agree with the LXX) and of Greek political, legal, and commercial terminology (e.g., Gal 3:24-25; Phil 3:20; Col 2:14).

3. Christian Tradition

   Clear evidence of Paul's dependence on apostolic tradition is supplied by the regular appearance in his letters of kerygmatic fragments (e.g., Rom 1:2-4; 10:8-9), liturgical fragments (e.g., Rom 11:33-36), catechetical or paraenetic passages (e.g., 1 Cor 6:9-10), historical summaries (e.g.,

III. TEACHING OF PAUL

Gal 4:4), Palestinian prayers (e.g., 1 Cor 16:22; Gal 4:6), and christological hymns (Phil 2:6-11; Col 1:15-20; 1 Tim 3:16). See also 1 Cor 11:2, 16, 23-24; 15:3-5.

4. Damascus Encounter with Christ

Pauline theology is essentially "the explication of the content of his conversion, the systemization of the Christophany."[1] The revelation Paul received at his conversion (Gal 1:11-12, 16) contained in embryo all his subsequent spiritual insights (see 1 Cor 9:1; 15:8; 2 Cor 4:6; Phil 3:12).

5. Apostolic Experience

While the boundaries of Paul's spiritual horizons were marked out at his conversion, only the passage of time and the compulsive effect of circumstances experienced during his pastoral ministry enabled him to encompass some of those horizons within his theology.

6. Progressive Illumination of the Holy Spirit

Paul's teaching was "in words taught by the Spirit, explaining spiritual realities with Spirit-taught words" (1 Cor 2:13 NIV). When the teaching of Jesus was not available to settle an issue, Paul was given divine illumination (e.g., 1 Cor 7:10, 12, 40).

B. The Godhead

1. The Trinity

Although the term "Trinity" appears nowhere in the NT, it accurately reflects the implied interrelationship between three distinct persons: the Father, Jesus Christ his Son, and the Holy Spirit, each equally sharing in the divine essence. This is apparent in Paul's three "overlapping binitarianisms" (an expression of R. R. Williams):

(a) God and Jesus Christ, as in 2 Cor 1:2

---

1. H. J. Holtzmann, source unknown.

(b) God and the Spirit, as in 1 Cor 2:11

(c) Jesus Christ and the Spirit, as in Rom 1:4

When Paul refers to all three persons together (2 Cor 13:14 = 13:13 in the Greek text; Gal 4:6), the term "God" (*theos*) refers to the Father, although on occasion (Rom 9:5 and Titus 2:13) *theos* can refer to Jesus Christ.[2]

2. God as Father

On thirty-three occasions Paul directly links the terms "God" (*theos*) and "Father" (*patēr*) (e.g., 1 Cor 1:3). In this combination *patēr* invariably follows *theos*: the word "God" is being defined in terms of fatherhood.

God is the Father of all persons in a creatorial sense (1 Cor 8:6; Eph 3:14–15; 4:6) but not in a redemptive sense, where he is exclusively the Father of believers in his Son (Rom 8:15–16; 2 Cor 6:17–18; Gal 4:6; Col 1:12–13).

3. God as Savior

In the Pastoral Epistles Paul five times speaks of "God our Savior" (1 Tim 1:1; 2:3; Titus 1:3; 2:10; 3:4), once declaring that this Savior God "wants all people to be saved" (1 Tim 2:4) where the expression "all people" (*pantas anthrōpous*) whom God desires to save and "to bring to a knowledge of the truth" refers to both "all without distinction" (based on race, status, or condition) and "all without exception." "There is universalism in the scope of redemption, since no person is excluded from God's offer of salvation, but there is a particularity in the application of redemption, since not all persons appropriate the benefits afforded by this universally offered salvation."[3] God is potentially the Savior

---

2. See M. J. Harris, *Jesus as God: The New Testament Use of* Theos *in Reference to Jesus* (Eugene, OR: Wipf and Stock: 2008) 45–46, 143–85, 269–99.

3. M. J. Harris, "2 Corinthians," in *The Expositor's Bible Commentary*, ed. Tremper Longman III and David E. Garland (Grand Rapids: Zondervan, 2008) 11:479.

of all, but actually the Savior only of those who choose to appropriate those benefits.

Romans 8:29-30 delineates the five successive stages in God's provision of salvation.

(a) **Foreknowledge** (*proginōskō*, "choose beforehand") is God's fixing of his affectionate regard on humans with a view to selecting them for a special purpose. It is more than advance knowledge but less than predestination.

(b) **Predestination** (*proorizō*, "decide upon beforehand, predetermine, foreordain") is God's appointment of humans to a special destiny—here defined as conformity to the image of Christ (or adoption into God's family, Eph 1:5).

(c) **Calling** (*kaleō*, "call") is God's choice of particular humans for the receipt of a special benefit—conversion and regeneration.

(d) **Justification** (*dikaioō*, "pronounce to be righteous") is God's judicial act of declaring righteous those who believe in Jesus Christ, on the basis of the atoning death of Christ and not law-keeping.

(e) **Glorification** (*doksazō*, "glorify, clothe in splendor") is God's elevation of believers to share in Christ's resurrection and exaltation.

4. Jesus Christ: His Person

(a) His humanity

Historically, and for good reason, the real humanity of Jesus has rarely been questioned. In the second and third centuries the Docetists (from *dokeō*, "seem, appear [to be]") taught that Jesus merely seemed or appeared to be human or to have a human body, appealing to passages such as 1 Cor 15:45 where the last Adam is spoken of as "a life-giving spirit," or 1 Cor 15:47 where Paul says the second man is "from heaven," or Rom 8:3 where God sent his Son "in the likeness of sinful flesh."

Paul is unambiguous on this point. Jesus was a descendant of David "as to his earthly life" (*kata sarka*, NIV), and as the one mediator between God and humankind Christ Jesus was "himself human" (1 Tim 2:5 NRSV) (cf. Rom 5:15; 2 Cor 10:1). Moreover, from the Israelites "is traced the human ancestry of the Messiah" (Rom 9:5 NIV).

(b) His deity

That Paul regarded Jesus Christ as sharing in the divine nature is clear from three considerations.

(i) **Divine status** is accorded to Jesus: as the possessor of divine attributes (Eph 4:10; Col 2:9); as being eternally existent (1 Cor 10:4; Phil 2:6; Col 1:17); as a joint possessor (with God) of the Spirit (Rom 8:9) and the kingdom (Eph 5:5); as universally supreme (Rom 9:5; 14:9; Eph 1:20–22; Col 1:17); as the perfect revelation of God (Col 1:15); as the recipient of praise and worship (Eph 5:19; Phil 2:9–11); as the addressee in prayer (1 Cor 1:2; 16:22; 2 Cor 12:8); as the object of saving faith (Rom 10:12); as the joint source of blessing (1 Cor 1:3; 1 Thess 3:11; 2 Thess 2:16); as the object of doxologies (2 Tim 4:18).

(ii) **Divine functions** are performed by Jesus: as the creator and sustainer of all nature (Col 1:16–17); as one who forgives sins (Col 3:13); as one who grants salvation or eternal life (1 Thess 1:10; Titus 1:4; 2:13; 3:6); as one who exercises judgment (Rom 14:10; 2 Cor 5:10).

(iii) The **divine title** "God" is used of Jesus: "to them [the Israelites] belong the patriarchs, and from them, according to the flesh, comes the Messiah, who is over all, God blessed for ever. Amen" (Rom 9:5 NRSV); "while we wait for the blessed hope—the glorious

III. TEACHING OF PAUL

appearing of our great God and Savior, Jesus Christ" (Titus 2:13 NIV).[4]

(c) His subordination to the Father

In addition to defending the equality of Jesus Christ with God the Father, Paul teaches the eternal subordination of Jesus to his Father. This subordination was not only during Jesus's earthly life, when he was obedient to his Father (Phil 2:8), but will be true at the end and beyond, when he will be subject(ed) to his Father (1 Cor 15:28). This explains why the apostle can say "Christ belongs to God" (1 Cor 3:23 NASB, NRSV), "God is the head of Christ" (1 Cor 11:3 NASB, NRSV), and "the God of our Lord Jesus Christ" (Eph 1:17; cf. 1:3), and also can affirm that the worship of Jesus as Lord promotes the glory of God the Father (Phil 2:10-11).

(d) His primacy as the Lord (Kyrios)

(i) over creation and all things

Christ is not only the creator of the universe (Col 1:16) but also its sustainer (Col 1:17), and is supreme over all things, animate or inanimate (Rom 9:5; Eph 1:21).

(ii) over the church

By God's appointment Christ exercises supreme headship over all matters relating to the church (Eph 1:22; cf. 4:15-16; 5:23-24; Col 1:18; 2:19).

(iii) over all people

Christ is Lord over all humans, whether living or dead (Rom 14:8-9) and the Master of believers who are his willing slaves (Eph 6:6).

---

4. See further M. J. Harris, *Jesus as God: The New Testament Use of* Theos *in Reference to Jesus* (Eugene, OR: Wipf and Stock, 2008), especially 315-17 (reflected in the above summary).

5. Jesus Christ: His Work as the Father's Agent

(a) Justification

This is a central concept in Paul's view of salvation (e.g., Rom 3:26; 5:1, 9; 8:33; Gal 2:16 (three times); 3:11, 24; Titus 3:7). The Greek verb *dikaioō* ("justify") means "declare righteous" rather than "make righteous."

This is because -*oō* verbs derived from an adjective that has a physical sense are factitive or causative in meaning (e.g., *doulos*, "enslaved," thus *douloō*, "enslave"), while -*oō* verbs derived from an adjective having a moral sense are putative in meaning (e.g., *dikaios*, "righteous," thus *dikaioō*, "declare righteous").[5]

Justification is not a decree of acquittal (which implies non-guilt), but is God's declaration of righteousness, the believer's acquisition of a new, right, and permanent relationship with God, based on Christ's propitiatory sacrifice (see d below). The sinner, who is guilty, has been absolved from the just consequences of their sin.

Justification is by grace (*tē chariti*, Rom 3:24), through faith (*pistei*, Rom 3:28; *ek pisteōs*, Rom 3:30; 5:1; Gal 2:16; *dia* [*tēs*] *pisteōs*, Rom 3:30; Gal 2:16), and evidenced by works (Gal 5:6; Eph 2:10; 1 Thess 1:3). Grace is the ultimate cause, faith the effective means, and works the natural and necessary concomitant of justification.

(b) Bearer of God's Wrath

"The wrath of God" has been understood in two basic ways: as an *affectus* ("emotion," "feeling"), the personal reaction of God to sin, his holy and eternal recoil against all that is evil; or as an *effectus* ("outworking," "execution"), an impersonal retributive principle, the automatic operation of cause and effect in morality throughout the universe. In favor of the

---

5. J. H. Moulton and W. F. Howard, *A Grammar of New Testament Greek* (Edinburgh: T&T Clark, 1919) 2:397.

former view is Paul's conviction that God is the personal author *and* executor of the moral law (Acts 17:24, 26, 28; Rom 1:20, 28, 32; 2:2-3, 6, 8, 15); and that the expression "enemies (of God)" (Rom 5:10; Col 1:21) implies feeling as well as the fact of opposition.

On the cross Christ canceled the legal indebtedness that stood against sinners (Col 2:14) and had incurred God's wrath. Similar sentiments are expressed in Gal 3:13 where Paul affirms that Christ became the bearer of the divine curse pronounced by the law (Deut 21:22-23; 27:26), and in 2 Cor 5:21: God caused Christ, the sinless one, to be "sin," thereby totally aligning him with sin and its dire consequence of being under the wrath of God.

(c) Substitution

Although Paul never explicitly says "Christ died in our place" (*anth' ēmōn = anti hēmōn*), he does say "Christ died for us" (*hyper hēmōn*, Rom 5:8; similarly Rom 5:6; 14:15; 2 Cor 5:14-15; Gal 3:13; 1 Thess 5:10; 1 Tim 2:6), probably because the preposition *hyper*, unlike *anti*, could simultaneously express both representation ("on our behalf") and substitution ("in our place").[6]

(d) Propitiation and Expiation

In Rom 3:25 the word *hilastērion* may be an adjective, "propitiatory/expiatory," with "sacrifice" (*thyma*) understood, or a neuter noun, meaning either "the means of propitiation/expiation" or (better) "a propitiatory/expiatory sacrifice." In English "propitiate" means "appease" or "make gentle in manner," while "expiate" means "make amends for" or "pay the penalty of." God is propitiated and sin is expiated; propitiation is through expiation. In other terms, God's wrath was averted when Christ atoned for sin.

---

6. See further M. J. Harris, *Prepositions and Theology in the Greek New Testament* (Grand Rapids: Zondervan, 2012) 50-51, 210-16.

(e) Reconciliation

This is the divine act by which, on the basis of the death of Christ, God's holy displeasure against the human race was appeased, the enmity between God and humans was removed, and humans were restored to proper relations with God (Rom 5:10–11; 2 Cor 5:19–21; Col 1:21–22). The evangelistic appeal "Get reconciled to God" (2 Cor 5:20) is the message of reconciliation and is the God-designed link between the objective work of reconciliation (an accomplished fact) and its subjective appropriation by sinners (a continuing process) (2 Cor 5:19–20). As an objectively real fact involving the entire universe (*ta panta*), reconciliation was actually achieved through Christ's death (Col 1:19–20).

(f) Forgiveness

This is the non-imputation of sin to sinners (2 Cor 5:19, "not counting people's sins against them"; Rom 4:7–8, citing Ps 32:1–2), because of its imputation to Christ (2 Cor 5:21). When God forgives sin, he does not forget or overlook it; rather, he chooses not to reckon it to the individual's account. Through the death of Christ, human sins (regarded, as it were, as "objects") are covered up and so removed from God's sight (Rom 4:7; cf. Ps 103:12); or human sins (regarded as debts owed to God) are canceled (Col 2:13–14; cf. Ps 51:1). So forgiveness can be viewed as the removal or cancellation of sins.

Whereas Jesus stressed that believers must forgive in order to be forgiven (Matt 6:12, 14–15), Paul emphasizes that believers are to forgive because they have been forgiven (Eph 4:32; Col 3:13).

(g) Adoption

In Paul's usage the word *huiothesia* (literally, "placement as sons/children," with no gender specificity) refers to the status of sonship resulting from the act of adoption. All five

III. TEACHING OF PAUL

NT uses of the term are Pauline (Rom 8:15, 23; 9:4; Gal 4:5; Eph 1:5) and show that adoption is both present and future. J. I. Packer suggests that the message of the NT is essentially "adoption through propitiation."[7]

(h) Principalities and Powers (KJV)

Although created by Christ as personal, supernatural agencies (Col 1:16), the "rulers and authorities" (*archai kai exousiai*, Col 1:16 NASB, NIV) are, as a consequence of their fall (implied in Col 1:20), evil potentates whose demonic aim is to enslave and deceive the human race (Col 2:20-22; Gal 4:3, 9; 2 Cor 11:13-15; 1 Tim 4:1). But through the cross of Christ they were disarmed and rendered helpless (Col 2:15; Eph 4:8), so that, although they remain active as "rulers" (*archontes*, 1 Cor 2:6, 8) or "cosmic powers " (*kosmokratores*, Eph 6:12) operating on behalf of Satan, "the god of this world" (2 Cor 4:4) and "the ruler of the spiritual powers of the air" (Eph 2:2), they are a defeated foe beneath the headship of Christ (Col 2:10).

(i) Summary

These crucial ingredients of Christ's work as God's agent may be summarized as follows. As the result of Jesus's bearing of God's wrath against human sin in the place of sinners and as an act of propitiation, God declares believers in Jesus to be righteous in his sight, the principalities and powers are defeated, the universe is reconciled to God, and sinners receive the forgiveness of sins and are adopted into God's family as his sons and daughters.

6. The Holy Spirit

(a) His Roles or Functions

(i) As the Spirit of God/Christ: Although Paul speaks of both "the Spirit of God" (e.g., Rom 8:14; 1 Cor 7:40) and "the Spirit of (Jesus) Christ" (Rom 8:9; Phil 1:19),

---

7. J. I. Packer, *Knowing God* (Downers Grove, IL: InterVarsity, 1973) 194.

there are not two distinct Spirits, but only one, who simultaneously "belongs to, emanates from, and represents God" (= "of God," a comprehensive or general genitive) and "belongs to, emanates from, and represents Christ" (= "of Christ," a similar genitive).

(ii) As the Spirit of Life: For Paul the Spirit is preeminently "the Spirit of life" (Rom 8:2; cf. 8:6, 10; 2 Cor 3:6), that is, "the Spirit who generates life," "the Spirit of invigoration"; his principal work is to produce new life, both physical and spiritual.

- In the case of the crucified Christ, the Spirit breathed life into his dead body. While this is nowhere explicitly stated in Paul's letters, there are unambiguous hints of this, as when the resurrection of Christ or his resurrection life is credited to "the glory of the Father" (Rom 6:4), God's power (2 Cor 13:4), or "the working of his mighty strength" (Eph 1:19–20). Then Rom 8:11 speaks of the parallelism between the Spirit's role in effecting Christ's resurrection and his role in raising believers.

- In the present age, believers serve God "in the new life provided by the Spirit" (Rom 7:6). Salvation comes "by the washing that produces regeneration and by the renewal brought about by the Holy Spirit" (Titus 3:5). The Spirit is the energizer of the believer's inner being (Eph 3:16; cf. 2 Cor 4:16).

- In the case of deceased believers, the Spirit will be God's agent in reviving their mortal bodies (Rom 8:10–11). Whether we read "through his [God's] Spirit" or "because of his Spirit" in v. 11, the role of the Spirit in revivifying the dead is clear. Then their resurrected body will be "characterized by power" (*en dynamei*, 1 Cor 15:43b), the Spirit's limitless energy. God's gift of his Spirit to believers is the pledge or down payment (*arrhabōn*) of their future resurrection transformation (2 Cor 1:22; 5:5; Eph 1:14).

(iii) Other Distinctive Roles: Other distinctive roles of the Spirit include his revealing of truth, viz. "the mystery of Christ" (Eph 3:4-5; cf. Eph 6:17; 1 Cor 2:10-13; 12:3), his indwelling of the church (Eph 2:22), his guidance and empowerment in prayer (Rom 8:26; Eph 2:18; 6:18), his creation of Christian unity (Eph 4:3), and his granting of spiritual gifts to church members (1 Cor 12:4, 7-11; 14:1, 12).

(b) The Baptism and Fullness of the Spirit

How these two different but complementary experiences of the Spirit are related may be illustrated by two pivotal verses, and by a chart that reflects the data of Acts as well as Paul's letters.

First Corinthians 12:13

"For indeed we were all baptized [by Jesus Christ, Matt 3:11] in the one Spirit so as to form one body—whether we are Jews or Gentiles, whether slave or free—and we were all given one and the same Spirit to imbibe."

Believers are in the sphere of the Spirit, and the Spirit is within believers. The Spirit is both around believers and within them.[8]

Ephesians 5:18

"Do not get intoxicated—that leads to sensual indulgence—but always be filled with the Spirit."

The verb "be filled" (*plērousthe*) is:

- plural—not a privilege reserved for the few
- passive in form—active yielding is implied

---

8. See further, M. J. Harris, *Prepositions and Theology in the Greek New Testament* (Grand Rapids: Zondervan, 2012) 230-31.

- present tense—continuous appropriation is needed

The present participles that follow the main verb ("be filled") indicate signs (see also Gal 5:22–23) of being filled with the Spirit: mutual edification (v. 19a), heartfelt worship (v. 19b), constant thanksgiving (v. 20), mutual submission (v. 21).

	Baptism in/with the Spirit	Fullness of the Spirit
1. Occurrence	single, unique, initiatory	repeatable
2. Mood	indicative only (seven times)	indicative *and* imperative
3. Tense	past, never future after Pentecost	past *and* future

C. Human Beings

1. As Bearers of God's Image

Paul explicitly refers to three successive stages in the relationship of humans to the image (*eikōn*) of God or of Christ who is the image of God (Col 1:15).

(a) A man (and, by implication, a woman; cf. Gen 1:26–27; Jas 3:9) bears the image of God (1 Cor 11:7). This original image was compromised but not eradicated by the fall, for although humans are by nature alienated from God and deserving of his wrath because of their evil behavior (Eph 2:1, 3; Col 1:21), they apparently retain that image, as the present participle (*hyparchōn*) in 1 Cor 11:7 implies.

(b) As a result of regeneration, the new self or inner person of believers is progressively transformed into the image of God or Christ "with ever-increasing glory" (2 Cor 3:18; Col 3:10).

III. TEACHING OF PAUL

(c) Believers' final destiny is to be fully conformed to the image of Christ, "the heavenly man" (Rom 8:29; 1 Cor 15:49).

In Christian theology the image of God has been located in a person's **nature** (as a self-conscious being who is capable of rational and abstract thought; as someone with moral responsibility); or in their actual or potential **relationship** (to God, as someone who can receive and respond to God's message; to other humans, in a harmonious and complementary way; and to creation, as a creator [as in procreation] and preserver).

2. Terms Describing the Human Person

   (a) Flesh (*sarx*)

   - bodily tissues (Rom 2:28; 2 Cor 12:7)
   - the physical body (Eph 2:14; Col 2:5)
   - human ancestry (Rom 1:3; 9:5)
   - humankind (Rom 3:20; Gal 2:16)
   - human nature, as weak (2 Cor 7:5; Col 1:22) or sinful (Gal 5:16–17; Col 2:11)

   (b) Body (*sōma*)

   - the physical body (Rom 12:4; Gal 6:17)
   - mortal embodiment (2 Cor 4:10; 5:6)
   - the whole person (Rom 12:1; Phil 3:21)
   - the self as sinful (Rom 6:6)

   (c) Soul (*psychē*)

   - life-principle, earthly life (Rom 11:3; Phil 2:30)
   - the individual person (Rom 13:1; 1 Cor 15:45)
   - the "self" (2 Cor 12:15; 1 Thess 2:8)

(d) Spirit (*pneuma*)

- the person in relation to God (1 Cor 7:34; Phlm 25)
- a synonym for "soul" or "self" (1 Cor 2:11; Gal 6:18)
- "mind" (2 Cor 2:13; 7:13)

There is clearly some flexibility in Paul's use of these terms; for example, *sōma*, *psychē*, and *pneuma* can each refer to the "self" (although with varying connotations).

What human bodies are by nature	What human bodies will become by grace
1. physical (1 Cor 15:44, 46)	spiritual (1 Cor 15:44, 46)
2. perishable, mortal (1 Cor 15:22a, 42, 50, 52–54)	imperishable, immortal (1 Cor 15:42, 50, 52–54; 2 Cor 5:4)
3. dishonorable (1 Cor 15:43a)	glorious (1 Cor 15:43a; Phil 3:21)
4. weak (1 Cor 15:43b)	powerful (1 Cor 15:43b)
5. earthly (1 Cor 15:47; 2 Cor 5:1)	heavenly (1 Cor 15:40, 48–49; 2 Cor 5:1–2)
6. from God via humankind (cf. 1 Cor 11:12)	directly from God (1 Cor 15:38; 2 Cor 5:1)

3. Being "in Christ"

Some see this expression (165 uses) as the essence of Paul's theology, equivalent to John's "in Jesus" (John 14:20; 15:4–7; Rev 1:9).

It has two basic meanings: *individual*, "in Christ" as an individual person, distinct from others (Eph 1:10; Phil 2:5; Col 1:19; 2:9) or "in (union/fellowship with the exalted) Christ" (Gal 3:28; Col 2:10; 1 Thess 4:16; 2 Tim 2:10)"; or *corporate*, "in (part of the spiritual body of) Christ" (Rom 8:1; 12:5;

III. TEACHING OF PAUL

Gal 1:22), where Christ is an inclusive or corporate person (cf. "Christ" in 1 Cor 12:12).

For the wide range of Paul's use of this phrase, see M. J. Harris, *Prepositions*, 123–24.

D. Images of the Church

1. In Relation to God the Father

    (a) The People of God (Rom 9:25; 2 Cor 6:16): composed of Jews and now also gentiles (Rom 9:24) who have been engrafted into God's olive tree (Rom 11:17–24). Together they constitute the new "Israel of God" (Gal 6:16).

    (b) The Temple of God: the sacred building or temple of the living God that he inhabits by his Spirit (1 Cor 3:9, 16–17; 2 Cor 6:16; Eph 2;21–22).

    (c) The Household of God: in which Jewish and gentile believers are fellow citizens (Eph 2:19; 1 Tim 3:15) and family members (Gal 6:10).

    (d) The New Humanity: that is being renewed by its creator (Col 3:10).

2. In Relation to Christ

    (a) The Body of Christ: where the emphasis is on the oneness of the body in spite of its many members and their differing functions (Rom 12:4–5; 1 Cor 12:12–13; Eph 4:4, 12; Col 1:18, 24; 3:15).

    (b) The Bride of Christ: where the emphasis is on the need for the bride's purity and sincere devotion to Christ, her one husband (2 Cor 11:2–3).

E. Sacraments of the Church

1. Baptism

    Paul regarded baptism as an acted parable, a dramatization of three central facts of the gospel—the death, burial, and resurrection of Christ (Rom 6:3-4). It was the believer's public identification with Christ in a death to sin (Rom 6:2, 5-6), a burial (Rom 6:4a; Col 2:12) that signified a break with the past (cf. 2 Cor 5:17), and a resurrection to new life (Rom 6:4b; Eph 2:5-6).

2. The Lord's Supper

Four expressions are relevant.

- The breaking of bread (1 Cor 10:16b; 11:23-24; cf. Acts 2:42)
- The Lord's Supper (1 Cor 10:21; 11:20)
- "Participation in the body/blood of Christ" (= Communion) (1 Cor 10:16)
- "The giving of thanks" (= Eucharist, from *eucharisteō*, "give thanks") (1 Cor 11:24; cf. 1 Cor 10:16a)

3. The Relationship between baptism and the Lord's Supper

	Baptism	Lord's Supper
(a) related to	water (Rom 6:4)	blood (1 Cor 10:16a; 11:27)
(b) mainly	individual	corporate in emphasis (1 Cor 11:18, 33)
(c) as a rite is	non-repeatable (Gal 3:27; 1 Cor 1:13; Col 2:12)	repeated (1 Cor 11:26)
(d) part of	initiation into the faith (1 Cor 12:13)	continuance in faith (1 Cor 11:28-29)
(e) means of	entry into a church	renewal in devotion (1 Cor 10:16; 11:24)

III. TEACHING OF PAUL

F. Ethics

1. Family Relationships

   (a) The Husband-Wife Relationship

   First Corinthians 7:3–6. It is the responsibility of each partner to fulfill their marital duties and meet the sexual needs of their spouse, and not seek their own self-gratification (vv. 3–4). Sexual abstinence within marriage should be only by mutual consent, temporary, and for a specific beneficial purpose (v. 5).

   Ephesians 5:22–33. The emphasis is on obligations to be honored, not rights to be asserted. The submission of wives to husbands (= recognition of their headship; cf. 1 Cor 11:3) is compared ("just as," *hōs*) to (a) their submission to the Lord (v. 22), and (b) the church's submission to Christ (v. 24). The love of husbands for wives is compared ("just as," *kathōs*; "in the same way," *houtōs*) to (a) their love of their own selves (vv. 28, 29a, 33), and (b) Christ's love for the church (vv. 25, 28a–29b).

   (b) The Parent-Child Relationship

   First Timothy 3:4–5. A father must manage his own family capably so that they respect him, remembering that conduct in one's own house prepares one for service in God's house.

   Ephesians 6:1–4; Col 3:20–21. Children are dignified with a special apostolic injunction that calls for their unswerving and total obedience to their parents as a way of pleasing the Lord. But parental training and instruction must be reasonable, to prevent their children becoming exasperated.

   (c) Relatives

   Christians have on obligation to support:

   (a) relatives by physical birth (1 Tim 5:4, 8);

(b) relatives by the new birth (Rom 12:10, 13; Gal 6:10b); and

(c) relatives in the sense of fellow humans (Gal 6:10a; 1 Thess 3:10).

2. General Human Relationships

At each level the Christian's primary obligation is the pursuit of peace and concord (Rom 12:18; 1 Cor 10:32–33).

(a) Interpersonal/Individual: basic principle—adopt an aggressive but qualified pacifism.

(i) A pacifism that involves (negatively) non-retaliation or non-vindictiveness (Rom 12:19–21; 2 Cor 13:4); and (positively) "neighbor love" (Gal 6:10) and "enemy love" (Rom 12:14, 21).

(ii) A qualified pacifism: "If possible, so far as it depends on you, live peaceably with everyone" (Rom 12:18; cf. Titus 3:2).

(iii) An aggressive pacifism: "Let us pursue what leads to peace" (Rom 14:19). "Make every effort to maintain the unity created by the Spirit by binding peace on yourselves" (Eph 4:3).

(b) Intra-Communal/Civic: basic principle—recognize a system of reward and punishment.

Paul affirms the God-ordained role of the state to punish evil and reward good (Rom 13:3–4) and calls for universal respect for rulers (Rom 13:3, 7; cf. 1 Tim 2:1–2) and for responsible submission to them for the sake of Christian conscience (Rom 13:1, 5; Titus 3:1)

Whereas in the personal ethics of Rom 12 the individual Christian is directed to "leave room for God's wrath" (Rom 12:19), in the social ethics of Rom 13 the judiciary is the executor of God's wrath (Rom 13:4). The right of exercising retributive justice that is denied to the individual is accorded to the state.

III. TEACHING OF PAUL

G. Eschatology

1. Death

   (a) Paul uses the terms "death" or "die" in three different senses.

      (i) *Physical death* generally denotes the irreversible cessation of bodily functions (Rom 5:12; 6:23) but occasionally it describes the gradual weakening of physical powers (2 Cor 4:12; cf. 4:16).

      (ii) *Spiritual death* refers to human natural alienation from God, lack of responsiveness to God, or hostility to God, because of sin (Rom 6:23; 7:9; Eph 2:1; Col 2:13).

      (iii) *Death to sin* involves the suspension of all relations with sin that results from being alive to God through dying and rising with Christ (Rom 6:4, 6, 11).

   (b) Nature of physical death for the Christian

      (i) *Destruction*, the dismantling of a tent-dwelling (2 Cor 5:1), involving the loss of physical corporeality (believers are no longer "in the flesh") and the loss of earthly corporateness (they are no longer "in Adam" but remain "in Christ;" 1 Cor 15:18; 1 Thess 4:16).

      (ii) *Departure* from mortal embodiment (2 Cor 5:8a; Phil 1:23; 2 Tim 4:6) to the presence of the Lord (2 Cor 5:8b; Phil 1:23). A departure implies a destination as well as an evacuation, a "to" as well as a "from."

2. The intermediate state

   This condition or period is called "intermediate" because it lies between two fixed points, death and resurrection, and because it is temporary, ultimately being eclipsed by the "final state" of humankind.

For believers it is a state of:

(a) *Consciousness.* As used by Paul (nine times, 1 Cor 7:39; 11:30; 15:6, 18, 20, 51; 1 Thess 4:13–15), the verb *koimasthai* does not refer to physical sleep, "be asleep" (as, for example, in Matt 28:13 or John 11:12) or imply unconsciousness or suspended animation after death, but it means "fall asleep" or "sleep the sleep of death." Christians who die "fall asleep" in that they cease to have any active relation to the earthly world of time and space, but they are fully alert to their new environment.

(b) *Bodilessness*, in which bodiless souls, in conscious communion with Christ, await the receipt of their resurrection bodies.

(c) *Enriched fellowship in the presence of Christ.* Immediately after death the Christian is "with" the Lord (*pros*, 2 Cor 5:8; *syn*, Phil 1:23; cf. *meta*, Luke 23:43), which refers to active interpersonal communion, not impassive spatial juxtaposition.

3. Resurrection

It is possible to distinguish four types of resurrection in Paul's thought.

(a) The past bodily resurrection of Christ from the dead to immortality (Rom 6:4, 9)

(b) The past spiritual resurrection of believers with Christ (Col 2:12)

(c) The future bodily resurrection of believers to immortality (1 Cor 15:52, 53–54)

(d) The future personal resurrection of the wicked (Acts 24:15)

In the first three cases resurrection denoted emergence from death (whether physical or spiritual) followed by a

III. TEACHING OF PAUL

radical transformation which in the first and third instances involves receipt of a spiritual/resurrection/heavenly body (Rom 6:5; 1 Cor 15:44, 48-49, 51) and the permanence of that new state (Rom 6:9-10; 1 Cor 15:53-54). Believers are "raised immortal" (1 Cor 15:52), which suggests that the transformation that results in immortality is coincident with the resurrection and in fact is part of the resurrection itself. And with resurrection comes exaltation. Believers will be raised up from the dead (revival; 1 Cor 15:42, 54) in newness of life (transformation; 1 Cor 15:51-52) into the presence of Christ (exaltation; 2 Cor 5:8).

4. Immortality

Only three NT terms express the idea of immortality; the first two (nouns) are exclusively Pauline.

(a) *Athanasia*, by derivation "non-dying-ness" = "deathlessness" (1 Cor 15;53-54; 1 Tim 6:16).

(b) *Aphtharsia*, by derivation "non-decaying-ness" = "incorruptibility" or "imperishability" (Rom 2:7; 1 Cor 15:42, 50, 53-54; Eph 6:24; 2 Tim 1:10).

(c) *Aphthartos*, "incorruptible" (Rom 1:23; 1 Cor 9:25; 15:52; 1 Tim 1:17; also 1 Pet 1:4, 23; 3:4).

The two nouns are complementary in meaning. A person who is immune from debilitating decay will therefore also be immune from death. And a person free from the inward working of the death-principle must also be free from its expression in decay.

Only God, the inexhaustible source of all life (Rom 11:36), is immortal by nature (1 Tim 6:15-16); humans become immortal by his grace. So immortality may be defined as the immunity from decay and death that results from having (in the case of God) or sharing (in the case of humans) the eternal divine life.

The ideas of resurrection and immortality are *inseparable*, since it is only by means of a resurrection transformation that the believer gains immortality, and the receipt of immortality is the inevitable result of experiencing a resurrection transformation (Rom 6:9; 1 Cor 15:42, 52-54). Moreover, the two concepts are *complementary*. A resurrection transformation guarantees that immortality is personal rather than ideal, racial, or pantheistic; is corporate rather than individualistic; and is somatic rather than spiritual. Also, Paul's teaching about immortality guarantees that resurrection is a continuing state rather than simply a single event, is a permanent rather than a temporary condition, and is a transformed state constantly sustained by God's life and power.

5. Comparison of Paul and Plato on Immortality

To highlight the distinctiveness of Paul's view of immortality, it will be helpful to compare his view with that of Plato.[9]

We shall compare a composite Pauline view drawn largely from his two Corinthian letters, and a composite Platonic view that draws particularly on the *Phaedo* and the *Phaedrus*. Plato was chosen for the comparison rather than any other ancient philosopher, not because the Platonic view of immortality was the dominant view in the ancient world even among the Greeks, but because of the epoch-making significance of Plato's arguments for immortality in the history of ancient thought and their widespread influence among Christian thinkers of all ages.

(a) Paul portrays immortality as a natural property of God, and of God alone (1 Tim 6:16), so that creaturely beings gain immortality only through relationship with him. But for Plato immortality was an inherent

---

9. The following draws on material that appeared in my book, *Raised Immortal: Resurrection and Immortality in the New Testament* (Grand Rapids: Eerdmans, 1985) 201-5, and is used with permission.

characteristic of the rational "part" or function of the human soul because of its affinity with the invisible, eternal realm of Ideas or Forms and because of its participation in the Form of life.

(b) In Platonic thought the individual person could lay claim to being immortal as a consequence of having a soul—the soul being tripartite (rational, spirited, appetitive). The immortality of a person's rational soul was an inherent and present possession, although only the true and unwavering philosopher could be said to be presently enjoying on earth the benefits of godlikeness (*Resp* 500D) and immortality (*Sym* 212A). But even when people prove themselves incurably guilty and so are condemned to eternal punishment in Tartarus, still the soul is not annihilated, for it never loses its natural property of immortality.

In contrast, Paul depicts immortality as a future acquisition. Believers will be "raised immortal" (1 Cor 15:52), that is, will be raised and so become immortal, not raised as they already are, immortal. They will "put on" immortality (1 Cor 15:53-54). Whenever the two terms that may be translated "immortality"—*athanasia*, "undyingness," and *aphtharsia*, "indestructibility" (see III.G.3) above)—are applied directly and personally to individuals (Rom 2:7; 1 Cor 15:42, 50, 52-54), the reference is always to a state that commences after death. Even those who equate immortality with eternal life and claim that the seed of immortality is implanted in the soul at the time of regeneration must concede the weight of this evidence and make the resurrection determinative for the full or the real possession of immortality.

(c) Plato regards humans as composed of two parts. The soul is totally distinct from the body, being (in its rational form or function) eternally pre-existent, incorporeal, invisible, and indestructible. Allied, therefore, to Plato's view of psychical immortality is a negative view towards the body. The body is governed by sensation and by desire for pleasure (*Resp* 1.328D; 2.380E) and since it is a contaminating impediment to the attainment of truth (*Phaed* 66B), like a shell in which an oyster is imprisoned (*Phaedr* 250C), it must be denounced and despised (*Phaed* 65C, D). Admittedly, a more positive view of the body occasionally emerges, especially in Plato's later works, so that a correspondence is recognized between bodily health and the wisdom of the soul (*Resp* 3.404E; 10.609C) and the body is seen as the instrument of the soul (*Tim* 42.E; 43A), but it remains true that the distinction between soul and body is not conceptual and relative but real and absolute. Human beings are incarcerated souls. Death severs the chains of the body, emancipates the soul, and makes possible pure intellectual knowledge (*Phaed* 65A, 67A). Only the emancipation from corporeality brought by death enables the rational soul to re-enter its true abode and breathe its natural air. Disembodiment is the ideal state of the immortal soul.

Whether we regard Paul's anthropology as basically monistic or decidedly dualistic, it cannot be said that he views the human body as the temporary joining of a pre-existent, immortal soul with a material, mortal body. Body and soul are united in an organic union, not associated in an external conjunction. The soul cannot be said either to reside *in* the body ("the ghost on the machine") or to *have* a body ("the tool in the hand"). So far from being the tomb or the tool of the soul, the body is the temple of the Holy Spirit (1 Cor 6:19), a member of the corporate Christ (1 Cor 6:15), and a living sacrifice to God (Rom 12:1).

III. TEACHING OF PAUL

This exalted Pauline view of human beings is consistent with his concept of death and the afterlife. Death is not welcomed as release from embodiment, although it does terminate the pilgrimage of faith (2 Cor 5:7–8) and inaugurate the vision of God (1 Cor 13:12). As for the believer's final destiny, Paul envisages it as somatic (1 Cor 15:35–54). Spiritual embodiment is the ideal state of mortal beings.

(d) It follows from Plato's repudiation of corporeality both in the here and in the hereafter, there is no room for the notion of the resurrection of dead persons.

For Paul (and all the writers of the New Testament) there is no incompatibility between the ideas of immortality and resurrection (see III.G.4 above). Immortality is gained through a resurrection transformation. And it is precisely this distinctive ingredient of resurrection that guarantees that immortality has a corporate as well as an individual dimension and relates to the whole person and not simply the soul.

(e) Whereas Plato saw immortality as the property of all human souls, Paul regards it as a conditional as well as a future possession. According to Paul, it is death or a propensity to death, not immortality, that humankind inherits from Adam (Rom 5:12; 1 Cor 15:22), and it is "those who belong to Christ," not all who are in Adam, who at Christ's coming will be made alive by a resurrection transformation that issues in immortality (1 Cor 15:22–23, 42, 52–54). Immortality is not a gift bequeathed to all by the first Adam but an inheritance won for the righteous by the second Adam. Possession of immortality is dependent on one's relation to the second Adam, not the first Adam.

(f) In the case of Plato, the ultimate ground for the assurance of immortality was belief in the soul's divinity, belief in its affinity with transcendent Being. For Paul, and, we may assume, all the early Christians, the basis of confidence that they would inherit immortality was the gracious will of God, who had already given them his Spirit as a pledge of a transformation that would result in immortality (2 Cor 5:4–5) and had promised immortality to those who sought it by perseverance in well-doing (Rom 2:7).

So pronounced are these differences between the Pauline and Platonic concepts of immortality that it is all too easy to overlook certain similarities, although even here it is usually a case of "similarity with difference."

- In both cases, hope for immortality springs from a religious sentiment, although Plato is alone in enunciating philosophical arguments to buttress the intuition or belief.

- In each case belief in immortality is a stimulus to sound thinking and right action. Plato saw people's supreme goal as the care of their immortal soul, their real self, to ensure its happiness in the world beyond. Paul links eschatology and ethics as he moves directly from a discussion of the doctrine of immortality into an exhortation to consistent and enthusiastic service (1 Cor 15:52–58).

- In Plato (*Phaed* 83E; *Resp* 613A; *Theaet* 176B), as in Paul, immortality involves "becoming like God," yet for the Christian this means conformity to the image of Christ (Rom 8:29; Col 3:10), rather than "a never-ending union with true reality," as in Plato.

- In both cases immortality is seen as personal, but in Plato immortality is "psychical" and incorporeal.

- Paul would agree with Plato that the earthly material body belongs to the world of mortality, but he would not agree that the body is alien to the soul and a dispensable element in real personhood.

The basic and irreconcilable differences between the views of Plato and Paul regarding immortality may be summarized this way.

	Plato	Paul
(i) immortality a natural property of	the rational "part" of the human soul	God alone
(ii) immortality regarded as	present possession	future acquisition
(iii) ideal immortal state	disembodied	somatic
(iv) immortality associated with	pure knowledge of Reality	resurrection
(v) immortality the (future) possession of	all human souls	"those who belong to Christ" (1 Cor 15:23)
(vi) assurance of immortality	belief in the soul's "divinity"(= affinity with transcendent Being)	possession of the Spirit as an *arrhabōn*

6. Eternal life

Whereas the apostle John depicts eternal life (*zōē aiōnios*) as both a present reality for believers in Jesus (e.g., John 6:47, 54) and a future experience (e.g., John 6:27; 12:25), Paul focuses on the futurity of eternal life—Rom 2:7; 5:21; 6:22–23; Gal 6:8; 1 Tim 1:16; 6:12; Titus 1:2; 3:7). In this phrase "life" denotes quality, not mere existence or biological life, but supernatural, spiritual life that comes from God and enables humans to share the divine life. "Eternal," on the other hand, denotes quantity, "with a beginning but without end," that is, "of unending duration," or "destined to last for ever."

As for the relation between Johannine eternal life, which has future and present aspects, and Pauline immortality, which has a negative (immunity from death) and a positive side (participation in the divine life), we may propose that eternal life is the positive aspect of immortality, and that immortality is the future aspect of eternal life.

7. Parousia/Second Advent

Several terms describe this personal and visible return of Christ to earth.

(a) *Parousia* ("advent") denotes the arrival of Christ on earth as a person of consummate dignity and authority (1 Cor 15:23, "at his coming;" 1 Thess 4:15), comparable to the ceremonial visit of a king or emperor to a province.

(b) *Apokalypsis* ("unveiling," "revelation") refers to the public revealing of Christ in his unparalleled glory (1 Cor 1:7; 2 Thess 1:7).

(c) *Epiphaneia* ("appearing") describes the sudden spectacular manifestation of the formerly absent Christ (2 Thess 2:8; 2 Tim 4:8).

(d) Occasionally verbs are used: he will "come" (1 Cor 11:26) or "appear" (Col 3:4).

In that Christ's second coming could occur at any time, it was "near" (Phil 4:5), being "perpetually imminent" but not temporally specified.

8. Judgment

(a) Sometimes God is said to be the judge (Rom 2:3, 5), sometimes Christ (1 Cor 4:4–5) or even his people (1

III. TEACHING OF PAUL

Cor 6:2-3) or angels (2 Thess 1:7). All people are to be judged, both the living and the dead (2 Tim 4:1), on the basis of their relation to Christ (Rom 5:9; 2 Thess 1:8-9) and their works during their lifetime (Rom 2:6).

(b) In the case of the righteous, who will appear and be examined before the tribunal of God (Rom 14:10) or Christ (2 Cor 5:10), their deeds are the outcome of their faith (1 Thess 1:3) and will determine reward or its forfeiture (1 Cor 3:8, 15; 4:5; 2 Cor 5:10), not destiny. In the case of the unrighteous, their deeds will seal their doom because they refused to obey the gospel of Christ (2 Thess 1:8).

(c) For Paul, then, the terms "judge" (*krinō*) and "judgment" (*krima*) may bear two senses: a judicial investigation that may lead to either a positive or a negative verdict; a negative verdict involving consignment to perdition.

9. The Final State

(a) Of the unrighteous

(i) Permanent banishment from God's presence (2 Thess 1:9)

(ii) Eternal retribution (Rom 2:8; 2 Thess 1:8-9)

In spite of passages that appear to use the word "all" in an all-embracing sense (e.g., Rom 5:18; 1 Cor 15:22), Paul does not express the view that all people will ultimately be saved (the non-believing after temporary punishment or a period of probation) (= "universalism"), as the immediate or wider contexts indicate (in the present cases, Rom 5:19 and 1 Cor 15:23). Nor does he teach that the unrighteous will be annihilated (immediately at death or after a period of punishment) (=

"annihilationism"), as if "eternal" (*aiōnios*) meant "in eternity" and not "throughout eternity" in 2 Thess 1:9.

(b) Of the righteous

The essential elements of Paul's view of the hereafter for believers may be summarized by six adjectives.[10]

(i) *Embodied.* The Christian's goal is not freedom from embodiment but a new form of embodiment. This new body will be:

- like Christ's resurrection body (Phil 3:21)
- of divine origin (1 Cor 15:38), with God as its architect and builder (2 Cor 5:1)
- heavenly (2 Cor 5:1–2), perfectly adapted to its new, natural habitat
- spiritual (1 Cor 15:44), that is, with a perfected human spirit animated and guided by God's Spirit
- imperishable/immortal (1 Cor 15:42, 52–54), free from decay and death
- glorious (1 Cor 15:43), with radiant and unsurpassed beauty
- powerful (1 Cor 15:43), with limitless energy and perfect health

(ii) *Localized.* Heaven is not only a condition—knowing and serving God—but also a place, where creation itself is liberated from its previous bondage to the law of decay and enjoys a freedom from birth-pangs by a glorious rebirth (Rom 8:20–22).

(iii) *Personal.* When believers' "lowly," earthly bodies are transformed into glorious, heavenly bodies

---

10. Drawn from my article "The New Testament View of Life After Death," *Themelios* 11 (1986) 47–52, used with permission.

like Christ's (1 Cor 15:47–49; Phil 3:21), personal identity and individuality are preserved, not eradicated by absorption into the divine: "God will raise *us* up" (1 Cor 6:14); "*we* await eagerly . . . the redemption of our bodies" (Rom 8:23). One and the same "person" finds expression in two successive but different types of body.

(iv) *Corporate* and *Active*. In the expression "we will be with the Lord forever" (1 Thess 4:17b), "we" encompasses all believers as a corporate group—those alive at Christ's return (1 Thess 4:15, 17; also 1 Cor 15:51) and those who are raised at that time (1 Thess 4:14–16; also 1 Cor 6:14; 15:52)—and "with" implies active, unmediated, interpersonal fellowship (as also "with" in 2 Cor 5:8; Phil 1:23), not merely personal juxtaposition. The life of the age to come is not a passive, individualistic union with God.

(v) *Permanent*. After their bodily transformation (1 Cor 15:51) and receipt of "an eternal house in heaven" (2 Cor 5:1), believers will be free of decay and death (1 Cor 15:42, 50, 52–54) and will experience a perennial rejuvenation (1 Cor 15:43) that will equip them for the enjoyment and service of God forever.

H. Paul and the Law

1. Paul's use of the term (*ho*) *nomos* ("[the] law") is varied: the OT (Rom 3:19), the Pentateuch (Rom 3:21), Mosaic law (Rom 2:13–14), the Decalogue (Rom 2:20–22), a specific Mosaic law (Rom 7:2; 1 Cor 9:9), law in any form (Rom 3:20; 7:12); "principle" (Rom 8:2), "tendency" (Rom 7:21, 23). No consistent distinction can be maintained between *nomos* and the articular *ho nomos*, as if between the principle of law/legalism (*nomos*) and the

Mosaic code (*ho nomos*). Usage in Rom 7:7–12 establishes this point.

2. For Paul observance of the law ideally or potentially could bring life (Rom 7:10; 10:5) but actually it never did (Gal 3:21; Rom 7:18) since it afforded a bridgehead for sin (Rom 7:5, 8, 11). While law-keeping can never be a means of justification (Rom 3:20–21; 9:31; Phil 3:9; Gal 3:10–12), the law remains "holy, just, and good" (Rom 7:12, 16) as "the embodiment of knowledge and truth" (Rom 2:20). Rom 10:4 may be rendered "Christ has brought the law to an end in its connection with (*eis*) righteousness in the case of everyone who believes" (cf. Rom 9:30–31). Justification "by faith apart from works" (Rom 3:28) sets law on its true base (Rom 3:31).

3. A distinction may be drawn between the ceremonial law "with its commands and regulations," which has been set aside (Eph 2:15), and the moral law as an expression of the character and will of God that remains valid. The law of Christ (1 Cor 9:21; Gal 6:2) or the law of the Spirit (Rom 7:6) is the law of neighborly love (Rom 13:8–10) and replaces the law of Moses as the guiding principle in the life of the believer.

4. During post-exilic Judaism the "reacting nomism" of pre-exilic Judaism (law-keeping as a result of election) continued, but there was also an "acting legalism" (law-keeping as the basis of obtaining righteousness and election). These two categories are proposed by R. N. Longenecker.[11] It is this legalism, the reliance on "the works of the law" to gain a right standing before God, that the apostle rejects (Rom 3:28; 4:2; Gal 2:16; 3:10–11).

I. Paul and Israel

1. The historical dimension (Acts)

---

11. Richard N. Longenecker, *Paul: Apostle of Liberty* (New York: Harper, 1964) 78–79.

III. TEACHING OF PAUL

(a) As a pre-conversion persecutor of "the church of God" (1 Cor 5:9; cf. 1 Tim 1:13), Paul tried to defend the religious purity of Israel (Acts 9:1–2).

(b) After his conversion he disputed with the Hellenists (Acts 9:29) regarding the messiahship of Jesus (cf. Acts 9:20, 22).

(c) He attended the Council of Jerusalem (Acts 15:12), where he must have concurred with the apostolic decision not to impose circumcision on believing gentiles either to gain or maintain salvation (Acts 15:19; 16:4), although he initiated the circumcision of Timothy for utilitarian reasons (Acts 16:3).

(d) He regularly argued in the synagogues, seeking to establish from the Scriptures that Jesus was the Messiah (Acts 13:14–41; 17:1–3; cf. 26:22–23; 28:23).

(e) It was rumored that he taught Jews "to forsake Moses" (Acts 21:20–21), although he was sensitive to Jewish scruples (Acts 21:21–26).

(f) He observed Jewish festivals (Acts 20:16; 24:11), and, even as a Christian, he claimed to be true to Pharisaism (Acts 23:6; 26:5; cf. Phil 3:5–6); the God of his fathers (Acts 24:14; 26:6); his nation (Acts 24:17; 26:7); and the customs of his fathers (Acts 28:17).

(g) He construed his appeal to Caesar (Acts 25:11), not as a repudiation of theocracy and Israel but only as an exit from Jewish intrigue (Acts 28:17–19; cf. 21:27–36; 23:12–22; 24:27; 25:2–3, 8–11, 24–25).

2. The theological dimension (Paul's letters)

(a) Paul distinguishes physical or national Israel (1 Cor 10:18), his "kinsmen by race" (Rom 9:3), from spiritual or true Israel (Rom 9:6b; cf. Rom 2:28–29; Phil 3:2–3), his kinsmen by spirit (cf. 2 Cor 5:16–17).

(b) He never repudiated his Jewish heritage (Rom 9:4-5; 11:1; 2 Cor 11:22; Phil 3:4-5; Acts 22:3; 26:4-5) but rather prayed and worked for the salvation of his kinsmen (Rom 9:1-3; 10:1).

(c) In sinnership and salvation, and therefore within the church, he recognized no distinction between Jew and Greek (Rom 3:9, 22-23, 29-30; Eph 2:14-16), but rather their equality (Gal 3:26-29; Col 3:11). Yet Jewish national identity, as determined by circumcision, remains (Rom 4:11-12; 9:24).

(d) Two important passages

Galatians 6:16

After the first part of the verse ("Peace and mercy to/ upon all who follow this rule"), two basic translations are possible: (i) "—to the Israel of God" (NIV, 2011); they are the new people of God" (NLT); or (ii) "and upon the Israel of God" (KJV, NASB, NRSV).

In the first case, "the Israel of God" is the church, "the true circumcision" (Phil 3:3), "Abraham's offspring" (Gal 3:29). In the second case, two groups are specified, one being all those who follow the "rule," the other ("the Israel of God") being national Israel as a whole, or the righteous remnant of Jews (= Jewish believers). On either view, the "rule" or principle that should govern people's lives is the conviction that the inward new creation, not an outward rite, is what counts in God's sight (v. 15).

Romans 11:25-27

The "hardening" of "part of Israel" (= Israel apart from the "remnant chosen by grace," Rom 11:5) is temporary, for the salvation that has come to the gentiles will provoke "Israel" to jealousy and to receive God's mercy

III. TEACHING OF PAUL

(Rom 11:11, 14, 25, 30–32) when the Messiah returns to earth "from Zion" (Rom 11:26).

"All Israel will be saved" (Rom 11:26) may refer to:

(i) all the new/true Israel = the church (cf. Gal 6:16)
(ii) the sum total of the godly remnant of all ages
(iii) the righteous Jewish remnant of the end times
(iv) Israel as a whole that is alive at the parousia (rather than every Israelite of any time period)

J. Paul and Jesus

Any consideration of the nature of Christianity must address the central question of the relationship between Jesus and Paul, the two leading figures in this religion.

1. Paul's knowledge of the historical Jesus:

- **His life**—descent from David (Rom 1:3), birth and humanity (Gal 4:4; Phil 2:7–8), instituted the Lord's Supper (1 Cor 11:24–25), betrayed (1 Cor 11:23), appeared before Pontius Pilate (1 Tim 6:13), crucified (1 Cor 2:2, 8; 15:3; Gal 3:1; Phil 2:8), buried and raised from the dead (Rom 6:4; 1 Cor 15:3), appeared to his followers (1 Cor 15:5–8)

- **His character**—self-giving (Rom 15:3; 2 Cor 8:9; Phil 2:6–7), humble and gentle (2 Cor 10:1), exemplary (1 Cor 11:1)

- **His teaching**—citations (1 Cor 7:10; 9:14; 11:24–25; 1 Thess 4:15), allusions (e.g., Rom 12: 14 [cf. Matt 5:44]; Rom 13:9 [cf. Matt 5:43–44]; Rom 14:14 [cf. Mark 7:15, 18]; 1 Cor 13:2 [cf. Matt 17:20])

This knowledge about Jesus would not have come from personal encounter with Jesus but from tradition passed on by persons well known to Paul such as Mark (2 Tim 4:11) or

Peter (who was consulted or interviewed by Paul in Jerusalem, Gal 1:18 [*historēsai Kēphan*]).

How are we to account for the relative paucity of data in the Pauline letters concerning the historical Jesus? There are several possible explanations. (a) In Paul's letters what is assumed as known by his addressees remains unstated. (b) His letters are addressed to particular situations and are not intended to be comprehensive or exhaustive in any regard. (c) Central in Pauline theology is the death and resurrection of Christ, not his life. (d) The early church was not particularly concerned with a recitation of biographical details concerning Jesus, witness the relative silence about his pedigree, boyhood, and early manhood. (e) Paul was not a witness of the events of Christ's life, and preferred firsthand testimony.

2. Paul's one-time attitude towards the historical Jesus is reflected in 2 Cor 5:16. "From now on (= since his conversion) we regard no one from a worldly perspective. Even though we once viewed Christ from a worldly perspective, yet now we no longer do so." What Paul is repudiating is not knowledge of or interest in the historical Jesus, but his superficial pre-conversion view of Jesus as a messianic pretender. He now views Jesus as the exalted Lord, God the Father's plenipotentiary (cf. Phil 2:6–11).

3. There are three basic proposals regarding the relationship between Pauline and Jesuanic theology.

- Paul merely provides the technical basis for the teaching of Jesus; their theology is **virtually identical**, only the form of expression differs—members of God's kingdom become members of Christ's church.

- Paul wrongly interpreted and improperly developed the teaching of Jesus (**discontinuity**).

- Paul rightly interpreted the message of Jesus, providing a legitimate development of that teaching in the light

III. TEACHING OF PAUL

of Jesus's death and resurrection (**continuity**). This view, which is to be preferred, has been defended in detail by D. Wenham.[12]

K. Development in Paul's Thought?

The idea of development can refer to the advance of a person's thinking to new concepts that reflect a change of outlook and the repudiation of earlier expressions of thought. Alternatively, "development" can describe the application of ideas to new situations and challenges without involving the rejection of previous thought. In this latter sense we may investigate the possibility that Paul's thought developed.

Throughout his career Paul faced opposition to his ideas and challenges to his advice from a wide variety of sources, opposition and challenges that forced him to explore various implications of his basic, unchanging conviction that Jesus of Nazareth was God's promised Messiah who rose from an ignominious death to be exalted to universal dominion as God's eternal Son. This ever-increasing appreciation of the implications of the gospel should not be seen as in any sense a movement from immaturity to maturity or from uncertainty to certainty. After all, his extant writing dates from about AD 48 to 64, roughly corresponding to his age.

Here are examples of topics where his thought seems to have "developed." Also see above, I.A.2.b, "The Grouping of Paul's Letters. 3. Content," regarding successive principal emphases apparent in his letters.

1. Christology

   (a) The relation of the "head" to the "body"; in 1 Cor 12:21 the head is one of many bodily parts, whereas in Col 1:18 and Eph 1:22-23; 4;15-16; 5:23 only Christ is the Head while the church is his body.

---

12. D. Wenham, *Paul: Follower of Jesus or Founder of Christianity?* (Cambridge: Eerdmans 1995); D. Wenham, *Paul and Jesus: The True Story* (London: SPCK, 2002).

(b) The cosmic consequences of the death of Christ are adumbrated in 1 Cor 15:27-28 and Rom 8:19-23 but only become explicit in Col 1:20; 2:10, 15; Eph 1:10, 21-22.

2. Pneumatology

In 2 Corinthians (3:18; 5:5) and subsequently (e.g., Rom 1:4; 8:11, 15-17, 23; Eph 1:13-14; 4:30) the doctrine of the Spirit becomes more intimately related than previously to the concept of resurrection.

3. Eschatology

Paul's assessment of his own relation to the parousia seems to have altered from assuming he would be alive at that time (1 Thess 4:15, 17 and 1 Cor 15:51) to envisaging his own death before the parousia (2 Cor 5:1, 8; Phil 1:23). His dramatic encounter with death that occurred between the writing of the two Corinthian letters and is described in 2 Cor 1:8-11 probably accounts for this change of perspective and his theology of death found in 2 Cor 5:1-10.

L. Some Modern Images of Paul

Given the diversity of Paul's background and experience (Jewish, Roman, Hellenistic), it is hardly surprising that there has always been a wide diversity in the evaluation of his views and his influence. This is evident in the extensive range of modern assessments.

1. The Hellenistic Jew (F. C. Baur, A. Deissmann, R. Bultmann)
2. The Jewish Syncretist (R. Reitzenstein, W. Bousset)
3. The Diaspora Jew (C. G. Montefiore, H. J. Schoeps)
4. The Palestinian Rabbi (W. D. Davies, E. P. Sanders)
5. The Apostate Pharisee (A. F. Segal)
6. The Mediterranean Traveler (H. V. Morton, H. Metzger)

III. TEACHING OF PAUL

7. The Roman Citizen (W. M. Ramsay)
8. The Missionary Strategist (R. Allen, J. A. Grassi)
9. The Apostle of Liberty (R. N. Longenecker, F. F. Bruce)
10. The First Christian Theologian (V. P. Furnish)
11. The Herald of Salvation (M. J. Harris)
12. The Master Manipulator (M. D. Given)
13. The Apostle of God's Glory in Christ (T. R. Schreiner)
14. The Apostle of Persuasion (J. W. Thompson)

M. The Center of Paul's Teaching

In two recent books[13] John M. G. Barclay has argued that for Paul *charis,* as a central and multifaceted concept, is unconditioned, but not unconditional. That is, the indiscriminate grace of God in Jesus Christ is a free but demanding and transformative gift, given spontaneously without regard to the worth of the recipient, but demanding a warm response of gratitude and righteous living. Barclay's primary focus is on Galatians and Romans but his second book extends his treatment to other Pauline letters.

Sometimes the essence of Paulinism is found in Christology (for example, "Christ-mysticism" or "being-in-Christ"; so A. Schweitzer) or salvation (reconciliation; so R. P. Martin) or eschatology (the apocalyptic cosmic triumph of God; so J. C. Beker)

In a dictionary article on "Salvation" in 2000[14] I proposed that, simply expressed, the center or unifying theme or dominant emphasis or coordinating motif of the OT is "God's salvation in Israel" and of the NT is "God's salvation through Christ." As applied to Paul, my proposal is that the

---

13. John M. G. Barclay, *Paul and the Gift* (Grand Rapids: Eerdmans, 2015) and *Paul and the Power of Grace* (Grand Rapids: Eerdmans, 2020).

14. M. J. Harris, "Salvation," *New Dictionary of Biblical Theology*, ed. T. D. Alexander et al. (Leicester, UK: InterVarsity, 2000) 767.

center or essence of the apostle's theology may be expressed this way:

> God the Father's salvation accomplished through his Son, Jesus Christ the Lord, and applied by God's Holy Spirit

This summary reflects:

1. The securing and application of **salvation** as the center of Paul's thought.
2. The primacy of the **Father** in the scheme of salvation; Paul's theology is not only theocentric but more specifically patrocentric.
3. The supremacy of **Jesus Christ**, God's Son, the sole means of salvation.
4. The unique role of God's **Spirit** in communicating the benefits of salvation.
5. Salvation as a complementary Trinitarian enterprise.

Certainly, if there is a single word that takes us to the center of Paul's theology, it is *charis*. It cannot be coincidental that the term occurs at or near the beginning and the end of each of Paul's letters, forming *the opening chord and dying refrain of every Pauline symphony* (Rom 1:7; 16:20; 1 Cor 1:3; 16:23; 2 Cor 1:2; 13:13; Gal 1:3; 6:18; Eph 1:2; 6:24; Phil 1:2; 4:23; Col 1:2; 4:18; 1 Thess 1:1; 5:28; 2 Thess 1:2; 3:18; 1 Tim 1:2; 6:21; 2 Tim 1:2; 4:22; Titus 1:4; 3:15; Phlm 3, 25). Paul saw himself as a herald (*kēryx*, 1 Tim 2:7; 2 Tim 1:11) of this divine grace.

The wide range of the term's meaning is illustrated by its use in 2 Cor 8–9 where Paul's summons the Corinthians to complete the collection for "the poor" in Jerusalem. In these two chapters *charis* occurs ten times in six different senses.[15]

---

15. Reproduced from M. J. Harris, *2 Corinthians* (Grand Rapids: Eerdmans, 2005) 559–60, with permission.

III. TEACHING OF PAUL

(a) "Grace," referring either to God's unconditional kindness lavishly displayed (8:9) or to God's enablement, especially his enablement to participate worthily in the collection (8:1; 9:8, 14)

(b) "Privilege" or "favor," used of the honor or opportunity of participating in the offering (8:4)

(c) "Act of grace," denoting the collection itself as a charitable and generous act (8:6)

(d) "Grace of giving," referring to the virtuous act of sharing or of affording help (8:7)

(e) "Offering" or "charitable work," describing the collection as an expression and proof of goodwill (8:19)

(f) "Thanks," the verbal expression of gratitude for an act of benevolence (8:16; 9:15)

This latter sense reflects Paul's four principal uses of the word: (unsought and unmerited) benevolence (Rom 3:24; Gal 1:15), act of benevolence (Rom 5:15; Titus 2:11), gratitude for an act of benevolence (Col 3:16), the verbal expression of gratitude for an act of benevolence (Rom 6:17; 7:25). The first two senses refer to the divine character and action, the second two to the human response.

In a nutshell, then, Paul is the herald of God the Father's gracious salvation through Christ.

www.ingramcontent.com/pod-product-compliance
Lightning Source LLC
Chambersburg PA
CBHW030903170426
43193CB00009BA/724